Catching up With Your Spirit

The Pursuit of Excellence in Obtaining the Promise

Christopher R. Avery Sr.

xulon PRESS

Merriam-Webster's Collegiate Dictionary
(Eleventh Edition)

Merriam-Webster's Collegiate ® Dictionary, Eleventh Edition, principal copyright 2003
COLLEGIATE is a registered trademark of Merriam-Webster, Incorporated Springfield, Massachusetts, USA

The Pursuit of Excellence in Obtaining the Promise

Christopher R. Avery Sr.
Revealing Grace Ministries Inc
P.O. Box 1177
Snow Hill, North Carolina
Email: Pastor@revealinggraceministries.org
Website: www.revealinggraceministries.org

www.xulonpress.com

Dedication

*T*o my late father William Anthony Avery (A Levite) who through various fishing trips passed on many valuable lessons of manhood as he imparted to me the importance of knowing God, finding my purpose and not setting boundaries over my life. I found His strength in Godly quietness as his prayers touched lives.

To my late mother Carrie Retha Avery (A Prophetess) whom God anointed to direct and guide her children, those of natural birth and those she adopted in the spirit. She revealed to us, "walk according to God's word and receive the promise."

Together no superior parents could have been a blessing. They taught my siblings and me through example to love as God loves and to live life as He gave life to the fullest.

To My Heavenly Father, to my Savoir Christ Jesus and Holy Spirit who is a present keeper,

May these Kingdom words richly bless and encourage you.

Acknowledgments

I have always strived to achieve Gods perfect will for my life, aware that many who pursue life-long goals have rarely, if ever, obtained them by their own works. The words that I present to you have come by revelation and numerous prayers, but they also came through God, who placed me on a path to meet the right vessels, those who carried the gifts I needed to share wisdom and words of encouragement.

I wish to thank those who know and some who may never know the importance of the roles they have played in my life.

To my heavenly gift and promise in time my wife.

To my children who are all amazingly gifted.

To my sister's, brother and brother in-laws who have all truly been my warriors of the spirit.

To everyone I call friend and to every warrior in the Spirit, especially the honored elders of my life.

To every great man and woman of God who has taken the time to impart words of wisdom. Know I have been blessed by God's grace to know you. I thank you.

To those who have kept me in prayer as I pray, may the hands of the Lord continually be upon you all.

Contents

Introduction

One absolute fact about the word **Spirit** is that regardless of whatever definition you may choose to accept, it is an **"undeniable truth"** that we all have a spirit. The spirit, given from God's very breath, is the premier and unique part of man that enables him to communicate with God.

As men and women are undergoing a period of diverse circumstances, there is an impulsive shift in their spiritual capacity. Ranging from infancy to maturity and exposed soul to wayward spirit, all who experience this absence of communication or loss of spiritual contact during these most treasured times in their lives. **Overwhelmingly,** it is because they have acknowledged the **where, why** and **who's** of life as the path to their destiny.

Many times we are persuaded by events and or occurrences, and it seems that at these very times, the internal working of the body **"the**

spirit" leaps far beyond what we are physically capable of achieving. However, this is not so! We have the God-given ability to catch up with a part of us (our spirit) and overcome tough times, obstacles and barriers.

Instead of giving up, we must learn to "GET UP" and catch up with the spirit part of us which will lead us into victorious living.

The prophet Habakkuk was like many of us, gifted and destined to achieve, (Habakkuk means **"the embracer"** as in an encourager). We have all been embracers of truth and encouragers of faith, but what the enemy **shows us, tells us, or sells us** has slowed our advancement to our destiny. The book of Habakkuk is three chapters long with only fifty-six (56) verses. In this book is a written conversation between Habakkuk and God. Our conversations with God are comparable to the one God had with the children of Israel. We have learned and gained intelligent much like them. Now, we have become curious and even rude; we speak and hear what we want, instead of what God is saying, thus experiencing a spiritual disconnect.

Words, which you think are spoken to encourage, are spoken precisely to break your concentration and shift your focus. Remember this, "these words may interrupt your concentration for a moment but will never be able to break your connection and your spiritual connection to

God." These same comments cause actions that have affected many: moreover, these very acts or actions have caused many to suspend their apprehension or attempt to reconnect with their spirit, in other words, their pursuit in obtaining the promise.

We find God sends messages of direction through dreams because in the realm of slumber is His opportunity to speak to those who will not pay attention to signs. Armed with this spreadsheet of prospect, we launch forward daring to share. But in revelation, when your dreams are shared too soon, others will speak your end and will attempt to smash them (your dreams), and they will if you allow them too. In Joseph's case, the promise for the family was disclosed in a dream, and the family members rebuked him. Their anger was increased when he told them his dreams *Genesis 37:5* **(KJV)** *⁵And Joseph dreamed a dream, and he told it his brethren: and they hated him yet the more.*

Anyone from a family member to a close friend can be used. In Matthew Chapter Sixteen, Jesus had to correct Peter who was close to him for his actions and comments: **Matthew 16:22 – 23 (KJV)** *²²Then Peter took him, and began to rebuke him, saying, be it far from thee, Lord: this shall not be unto thee. ²³But he turned, and said unto Peter, Get thee behind me, Satan: thou art an offence unto me: for thou savourest not the*

things that be of God, but those that be of men.
Your dreams are your interpersonal conversation
with God. Until the revelation becomes reality,
hold it until the Lord's words come to release the
promise.

God told Habakkuk that the vision is yet for
an appointed time and that it would not tarry. The
connection was in revelation telling us, "GET
READY."

The prophet Isaiah teaches us some things
about catching our spirits; he first saw the angels
and cried, "I am not worthy," but when the angel
touched his mouth, He begins singing, "Send me
I'll go!"

The prophet articulated a catch phase which
was spoken twenty-five (25) times in the sixty-
six (66) chapters where he declares **"Holy One
of Israel"** which means in modern terms, **"He is
my God."**

It is all about two things: getting in shape and
the mental and physical preparation for pursuit.
Having a made-up mind to run and soar where
the spirit allows us to feel the breeze of what we
can acquire, which is the promise. "GET SET"

Finally, the Apostle Paul, while shackled to a
Roman soldier, writes *[14]I press toward the mark
for the prize of the high calling of God in Christ
Jesus. Let us therefore, as many as be perfect, be
thus minded: and if in any thing ye be otherwise
minded, God shall reveal even this unto you.*

We can pursue with heartiness and led by the excellence of the calling of Jesus Christ will enable us to obtaining the Prize, which is God's Promise.

One particular Sunday, I heard God speak as He directed me to look at the congregation which He addressed as **my children of promise.** I replied, "Yes Lord, I see them." His reply was **"you've seen them through your eyes; now see them as I do."** It was at that moment that my eyes were actually opened, and I saw the spirits of men and women, dejected, wounded and exhausted. I saw the spirits of people who were rejoicing, yet their physical man sat unaware, lethargic and uncaring. It was at that exact moment God spoke, and I first uttered the cry:

"People of God, catch up with your spirit and receive the promise!"

This is the exact time and opportunity because it is when God is giving us a glimpse. What's so special or promising about this glimpse or pause from reality, this commercial break, is that God, the author and finisher, has decided that you've complained enough, and become tired enough, must now stand still and let Him show you what's in store for you!

God allows us to glimpse our destiny, since we are by the very nature of the Godhead; His most gifted and created vessels. Chosen with a purpose we enter into this very inheritance of our bloodlines, prepared by God Himself. He has to give us a glimpse because we could not handle seeing the entire blessing. We would go around giving things away before they ever touched us in the natural.

While running for the Lord, we cannot take this race for granted. While we dance with youth and vigor, our dance is a break-through for someone, but it is also a spark of remembrance for the older saints. While some pray with extraordinary words, it is the moans and groans of the spirit that provide breakout moments. The Spirit is Creator, not consort **Genesis 1:2 (KJV)** *²And the earth was without form, and void; and darkness was upon the face of the deep. And the Spirit of God moved upon the face of the waters.* Moreover, according to **Psalms 104:30 (KJV)** *³⁰ Thou sendest forth thy spirit, they are created: and thou renewest the face of the earth.* The spirit brings power, focus and life. **Acts 1:8 (KJV)** *⁸But ye shall receive power, after that the Holy Ghost is come upon you: and ye shall be witnesses unto me both in Jerusalem, and in all Judaea, and in Samaria, and unto the uttermost part of the earth.* The spirit is your source of resurrection: **Ezekiel 37:5 - 12 (KJV)** *⁵Thus saith the Lord GOD unto* *these bones; Behold, I will cause breath to enter into you, and ye shall live: ⁶And I will lay sinews upon you, and will bring up flesh upon you, and cover you with skin, and put breath in you, and ye shall live; and ye shall know that I am the LORD. ⁷So I prophesied as I was commanded: and as I prophesied, there was a noise, and behold a shaking, and the bones came together, bone to his bone. ⁸And when I beheld, lo, the sinews and the flesh came up upon them, and the skin covered them above: but there was no breath in them. ⁹Then said he unto me, Prophesy unto the wind, prophesy, son of man, and say to the wind, Thus saith the Lord GOD; Come from the four winds, O breath, and breathe upon these slain, that they may live. ¹⁰So I prophesied as he commanded me, and the breath came into them, and they lived, and stood up upon their feet, an exceeding great army. ¹¹Then he said unto me, Son of man, these bones are the whole house of Israel: behold, they say, Our bones are dried, and our hope is lost: we are cut off for our parts. ¹²Therefore prophesy and say unto them, Thus saith the Lord GOD; Behold, O my people, I will open your graves, and cause you to come up out of your graves, and bring you into the land of Israel.*

When you begin this pursuit, know that the blessings that were prescribed just for you are pursuing you, and the Bible declares that they will overtake you. When you have prayed,

"Lord send a healing," there has to be an occasion where healing can overtake you. Sometimes needed afflictions come to trip you so they can do just that, overtake you.

God does not promise us the absence of hills and valleys in life, but His word does say, "We will walk through the valley." (Palms 23) When we come out, we will not be the same as we were when we went in. The Bible has over 1000 recognized promises and countless others spoken by God to men and women and their situations. If you would know the value of the promises and would take pleasure in them in your own heart, meditate much upon them. These promises are like grapes in a bunch. We find large beautiful clusters, and, always, the larger grapes are sought foremost while the smaller ones are ignored. One would be content after consuming larger grapes, but the smaller grapes are sweeter and can be enjoyed because we can have more. For that reason, seeing that the promises are the word of God, so true, so undeniable, so potent, and so wise, we must believe the promise even if it comes in small grapes. If we consequently meditate upon the promises and consider the Promiser, we shall experience their sweetness and obtain their fulfillment. As we walk day after day, month after month or year after year, we can pursue with excellence, and obtain the Promise. Now, go on, and begin your pursuit.

Chapter 1

Beginning the Pursuit

*~If ever I am to obtain success, I must acknowledge my
accomplishments to be of the measure of Grace
that God has enabled me to attain~*

(Part I) Actions and Inventories

The pursuit of your spirit, to begin with, will not be accomplished without difficultly. For this reason, many obstacles, both natural and spiritual, frustrate our paths. Some obstacles, which we have created by our thoughts, have become hindrances much like bars and barriers. The realization is that the mind, coupled with the creative speaking power (the authority) of the tongue, has allowed the very things that are invisible to gain control. This control affects our destiny, finances, relationships, and even worship.

In Scripture, Jesus said that **the Spirit is like the wind in that one cannot see it but**

one can see its effects: John 3:8 (KJV) *⁸The wind bloweth where it listeth, and thou hearest the sound thereof, but canst not tell whence it cometh, and whither it goeth: so is every one that is born of the Spirit.*

This is true of both the Spirit of God and the spirit of a human being. Our culture affects our Spirit in regard to emotions, attitudes, and intentions. Society consistently draws our awareness to an observance of calendar dates rather then days of biblical prominence. Such recognition creates obstacles.

One such occasion that has become most reflective is the birthing of the New Year, the transition or shifting period. It begins with the declaring of resolutions affecting your life and changes for the coming year, which we verbalize. Instead, it should be a time when the reflective events of your life's history should be considered because you have made it into another season. Although this particular event was not promised, it is one of many reasons to give thanks. Ponder this question: "How did you end the old year? What was your mindset as midnight approached, signaling the end of a year?

As we began the transition to another year or season filled with extraordinary potential, how many people, if any, conducted a personal inventory? Such an inventory considers what God saw in us and expected out of our walk. Remember,

"God is everything and in everything, you will find God". Some of your greatest lessons will be learned in your efforts to realize that who you are and what God has promised you will come. **When God says it, that settles it.** We are in no position to debate God's intention for our lives!

You may be wondering, "What about my prayers and walk with God and what He has brought me through in the closing of another year?" Remember how the Lord has kept you. If you would begin to conduct a personal inventory, the body should experience a spiritual quickening. It is one beyond the ordinary, the kind where you shudder and an unexplainable charge runs through you! The revelation that you would receive is that of a precept because a precept is a command or instruction intended to cause an action.

In *Psalms 119: 40 (KJV)* we read *"behold I have longed after thy precepts; quicken me in thy righteousness"* These words are instructions intended to cause an action and is so applicable to the people of God at all times. It alone is suited to strengthen the mind in the midst of trials and up-lift the soul. There is a value in the word of God that cannot be measured. In His instructions are truths and our heavenly Father's precepts. Prepare yourself, for God's answers will "Quicken you" with a glimpse of what is in store for your future and your spiritual pursuit.

(Part II) Stretching your thinking

God, the Father, will allow us the spiritual vision to see "the transition." This vision assists us in seeking a revelation for transition and for the transition of others. In the book of John, the fourth chapter has two particular verses which direct our thinking towards entering a new era.

John 4:23-24 (KJV) [23]But The hour cometh and now is, when the true worshippers shall worship the Father in spirit and in truth: for the Father seeketh such to worship him. [24]God is a Spirit: and they that worship him must worship him in spirit and in truth.

This era is one of the greatest known to humankind, but the church has allowed a spiritual uneasiness to creep in and grab hold. It has arrested our spirit in such a manner that we become uncomfortable both in and out of church. It has imprisoned our spirits with the traditions of other cultures and religions, so we have become unsettled and impatient.

This circumstance, although temporal, has caused a shift in our way of undertaking the biblical heritage which is given to us as an inheritance. What we should be reflecting on in this era is the truth. We will, by way of religion and cultural awareness, live the dreams and speak the words spoken as children of what and where we want to be.

In the story of the Samaritan woman at the well, we find a spiritual reflection of what brought her to her destination and our beginning instructions to **catching up with your spirit!**

As written she had traveled to a place of refreshing, maybe to nourish a need or to seek solitude from others. Yet, there is no reference to the distance or length of her journey. Therefore, by nature, habit, or need, she went to a place of inheritance, a place of heritage known to her as Jacob's Well.

Many times, the house of worship is our **well** a place of **nurturing** or **refreshing**, where we go for nourishment. But in truth, parents or friends constantly took us there, and it became a habit or a need because it is where we belonged. However, now it has become a place of solitude, isolation, and loneliness.

At the well sat Jesus who observed the woman approaching. He saw her weariness, perceived the many dilemmas of her past, and watched as she slowly and wearily continued. He has been watching many of us individuals under the same condition, almost too weary to attempt any form of pursuit.

In *John 4: 6(KJV)* it says*: "Jesus therefore, being wearied with his journey, sat thus on the well: and it was about the sixth hour."*

23

This particular passage is of interest, for it refers to **"the children of promise"**, those who have walked to the altar or those who paced around their houses or workplaces, weary, worn, and/or tired.

Does your situation even mirror those who have sat at home beating the arm of their favorite chair or on the edge of their bed? Some cry or pace around the house; there may even be waling. Then there are those who quietly and wearily make their journey to the well.

At the well is where this particular woman's transition occurs. In recognizing your transitions, consider the definition of a well: **"A place where a hole is dug into the ground to obtain a flow, surge, or a rush of water" Water refreshes, nourishes, and cleanses (the place of worship).**

Jesus is sitting and watching your approach. He has the best seat, at the right hand of the Father. **God says that your transition began to take place while you were praying, "Lord, heal me, prosper me, move me. Save my husband, wife, son, daughter, cousin or friend. I want to be closer to you. As you prayed the word, the Lord heard His voice and leaned over to hear you.** *Palms 121:4(KJV)* "He will not slumber or sleep, Jesus had His eye on you.*

Jesus, "The Lord", saw and heard you and knew that you had to exercise some faith. You had to walk, so He asked you to come all ye who are burdened and heavy laden. The woman at the well asked Jesus, "You brought nothing to get something out?" When Jesus asks you that same question in this new era, He loves us so much that He provides the answer:

²⁴God *is* a Spirit: and they that worship him must worship *him* in spirit and in truth.

God has sought you out and called you into fellowship with Him.

Often times through explanation, events, and or occurrences, it seems that the internal working of the body "the spirit" leaps far beyond what we are physically capable of achieving, but not so. We have the God-given ability to catch up with a part of us (our spirit) and overcome tough times, obstacles, and barriers. Instead of giving up, we must learn to **"GET UP"** and catch up with the spirit part of us that leads us into victorious living.

Come with that in mind, and it will allow you to reach the well. Debt, doubt, despair, sickness, loneliness, hurts, and pains have and will come. These are obstacles, not tricks of the mind. Here they are real, but they are the very weapons of the enemy to attack your spirit and to hinder you as you pursue your Spirit. God propelled your spirit into a season (year) of fullness:

(Part III) Invisible to Visible

God moved your spirit into a season of healing, health, and prosperity. While you were walking towards the end of last year, proclaiming

things had become commonplace or the thrill was gone, your spirit was stretching like a sprinter before a race. Meanwhile many were exclaiming, "I am tired, and I woke up tired." Your spirit was approaching the starting line. It is at very times like these when people are saying, "I am not being fed here" or "I have outgrown this teaching." Your spirit was digging in.

The very words (preaching or teaching) that held you together at your weakest or darkest hours were supplying you with nourishment. Your spirit holds it together. While the year was ending with you murmuring, wandering, lacking, and hurting in the natural, your spirit was rejoicing because God propelled it forward. Now inside of you it beckons, "Come on over baby; move Closer baby; you're almost there."

Those restless nights you thought would never end are over, and those tired morning feelings are now replaced with joy. Weeping may endure but for a night, but Joy comes in the morning. All you have to do is catch up with your spirit. Because as spiritual beings we fellowship with each other in spirit and reality, when we make contact with God through our spirit we will experience some of the greatest victories of our generation. Thus, when our light should be shining the brightest, we will not dim it with doubt.

Jesus told the woman at the well; *John 4:23-24 (KJV) [23]But The hour cometh and now is, when the true worshippers shall worship the Father in spirit and in truth: for the Father seeketh such to worship him. [24]God is a Spirit: and they that worship him must worship him in spirit and in truth.*

Her spirit leaped, and the Bible says, "She threw down her water pot and immediately left." The words of Jesus caused her to want to tell somebody else how to get that rush, how to **"Catch up with their Spirit.**

It is the moment our eyes open. The scales fall off, even on our jobs, in our households, and among our families. We clearly see what we had hurt, neglected, and abandoned. But I want everyone to rejoice and cry out the victory praise. What's been holding you back has been broken off of you now. People of God it's about to happen; you can Catch up with your spirit.

Now, understand that with God there are no excuses. When we base our principals on scripture, there are no excuses. The Creator would no sooner see us hindered by bars as He would allow us to remain in bondage. God continually provides spiritual direction for over-coming. God's words provide not just the file to saw through these bars, but the torch to melt them away with the purpose of allowing the invisible to become visible, all because of the word authority.

Chapter Four of the Gospel of John speaks of a man whom John preferred to identify by his title; "the nobleman." Even in various translations, you'll find that all references to this man's position refer to one having authority. This nobleman seeks a man called Jesus because he has heard that Jesus has done great things.

John 4:47-53 (KJV) ⁴⁷When he heard that Jesus was come out of Judaea into Galilee, he went unto him, and besought him that he would come down, and heal his son: for he was at the point of death. ⁴⁸Then said Jesus unto him, Except ye see signs and wonders, ye will not believe. ⁴⁹The nobleman saith unto him, Sir, come down ere my child die. ⁵⁰Jesus saith unto him, Go thy way; thy son liveth. And the man believed the word that Jesus had spoken unto him, and he went his way. ⁵¹And as he was now going down, his servants met him, and told him, saying, Thy son liveth. ⁵²Then inquired he of them the hour when he began to amend. And they said unto him, Yesterday at the seventh hour the fever left him. ⁵³So the father knew that it was at the same hour, in the which Jesus said unto him, Thy son liveth: and himself believed, and his whole house.

The last time Jesus was in Cana of Galilee, he changed water into wine. But like many of this lifetime, because you did not witness it, there is room for doubt, and he was relying on what spread by word to be true. Still, it was a crisis, an act of desperation; it was lost hope and hope lost which led the nobleman to seek Jesus. Today many of those who are in similar situations have heard about the goodness of Jesus, but are they seeking Him?

Mark 7:32 (KJV) reads, *[32]And they bring unto him one that was deaf, and had an impediment in his speech; and they beseech him to put his hand upon him. A crowd, who wanted to test a theory, sought a miracle and brought to Jesus one who was deaf.*

The centurion, a man of authority in a military environment speaks in **Matt 8:6** *(KJV): [6]And saying, Lord, my servant lieth at home sick of the palsy, grievously tormented.* He sought Jesus out of his faith.

We see a similar situation in the family of Peter in **Luke 4:38(KJV)** *[38]And he arose out of the synagogue, and entered into Simon's house. And Simon's wife's mother was taken with a great fever; and they besought him for her.* They do so because they knew He could it, Do you seek Him?

When dealing day-by-day with situations, has anything gotten under your skin, affected your family or way of life? There is a man who has the answers, and all you have to do is seek Him. Can you imagine this nobleman almost out of breath and at wits end looking around, asking people, "Have you seen Him? Imagine the puzzle look on their faces as this man of authority questions them and their reply, "Seen who?" Then imaginer, his cry, "Jesus, I need to find Jesus!" Have you cried that lately? If you need a moment, it's okay if you need to cry out, "I need you Jesus!"

There this man of authority was clinging to the arm of Jesus. He besought him, "Please come; my son is near death." There are some people facing dying situations and relationships, watching the terminations of jobs that will lead to an increase of struggling. Implore Him today. In the scripture, Jesus answer was the same yesterday as it applies today. We cannot continue to wait for a microwave experience. Jesus said, "Except you see signs and wonders, ye will not believe."

(Part IV) With a made up mind

We have been applying restraints to the unlimited wisdom and knowledge of God to suit our own way of thinking! The scripture says in

Matthew 17:20 (KJV) ²⁰*And Jesus said unto them, Because of your unbelief: for verily I say unto you, If ye have faith as a grain of mustard seed, ye shall say unto this mountain, Remove hence to yonder place; and it shall remove; and nothing shall be impossible unto you.*

We speak to the mountain on Monday morning at 6:00 a.m. and at 6:05 a.m., if it has not moved, we doubt God's word. We may check again at 7:00 a.m. and start remembering that our time is not Gods time. When we still see the mountain at 9:00 a.m., we begin to say, "Why Lord? Please forgive me. "You go to bed, and the next day the mountain is still there, so you question God more. Three days later, you give up hope! What you did not know was when you began to pray, the mountain began moving inch by inch. It is like some of those people we label "set in their ways," but the mountain started to move because God heard your prayer.

Jesus asked you to have faith the size of a mustard seed. The word says stand still and see, so why have you been running away? Stand on the promise. Jesus says, "Nothing shall be impossible unto you." I can do all things through Christ who strengthens me! Standing still and holding on takes strength to not give up. This nobleman became persistent and shamelessly began to plead to Jesus, "If you do not my child will die"

The word for that is **Importunity**, which is a persistent, selfless, and continual inquiry.

Acts 12:5 (KJV) [5]Peter therefore was kept in prison: but prayer was made without ceasing of the church unto God for him. **(We can do it) James 5:16 (KJV)** *The effectual fervent prayer of a righteous man availeth much.* **(We can do it)** Jesus looked at the nobleman and said, Go thy way thy son liveth." When you consider this, it should enlighten you with joy because when you know the Lord has answered your prayers, who could contain the joy? When you know that, you know.

These verses permit us to see the transition beginning but we need to know the meaning of a **nobleman or noblewoman.** One definition of nobleman is "**A person of rank and or birth, who is noble in any country**" according to Webster's. **Acts 7:6 (KJV)** [6]*And God spake on this wise that his seed should sojourn in a strange land.* They considered a **person or persons who frequent sovereign courts.** *Psalms 100:4 (KJV)* [4] *Enter into his gates with thanksgiving, and into his courts with praise: be thankful unto him, and bless his name.* The word **Sovereign** stands out.

Sovereign found in Webster's means "a person, group or body who has sovereign power or authority, who has supreme rank and power to the greatest degree, above in character or importance," The word of God declares **we are a royal priesthood, a peculiar people.** Moreover, that lets me know that we are sovereign. *Psalms 8:4 (KJV)* reads: *⁴ what is man, that thou art mindful of him? and the son of man, that thou visitest him? I'm Sovereign;* God says we have authority over all things. In addition, it gets better because when royalty gets together in the presence of the King, as heirs God has given us the authority to speak over those things and to intercede on the behalf of those who need prayer.

You are a child of God (A person). You are among the promise seed (part of a group). You are of the body of Christ. You might need to say when the enemy comes to kill, steal and destroy, "Under who's Authority!" Now, put it back (bring it back) with authority. The Bible records in *John 4:53 (KJV)* *⁵³So the father knew that it was at the same hour, in which Jesus said unto him, Thy son liveth: and himself believed, and his whole house.* The nobleman is referred to as father, the situation was reversed (death was defeated), and now the whole house believed.

The Authority that we receive has come through a matter of choosing. We dwell among a people who would no sooner see us prosper, but because we serve a God who would no sooner see us perish, we flourish. *Joshua 24:15 (KJV)* *¹⁵And if it seem evil unto you to serve the LORD, choose you this day whom ye will serve. whether the gods which your fathers served that were on the other side of the flood, or the gods of the Amorites, in whose land ye dwell: but as for me and my house, we will serve the LORD.*

The validity and reliability of God's word have assured us of success when we experience misunderstandings, difficult people, broken friendships, jealousy, and gossip. Do not allow these situations to become bars; you are of the promise. Break free and understand clearly. "You can declare, "I will live, I am healed, I will prosper, me and my whole house." Your spirit saw your hurts, pains, and you misunderstood as you were pulled towards victory and resisted. Now, with a new understanding pursue it.

Chapter 2

The Pains of Pursuit

~Who I am in the natural is seen by man, but who
I am destined to be is seen by God~

No athletes, particularly runners, (we are in a race) have ever trained to contend with the intention of failing; their ultimate goal is to win. Prepared through the aid of trainers (teachers) and coaches (pastors), they endure many grueling days and hours of training. The guidance and advice received is all in preparation for the day when the runners await the signal to begin the race. As they settle into the starters block, their only focus is on the official's instructions. In pursue of your spirit, the command is **"Get ready, get set, and go,"** and to us it has more significance then merely beginning a race.

In order to compete, we must train. Getting in shape will require not only the physical but also the mental preparation for pursuit. Having a made-up mind is a necessity, for you are about to reconnect with a part of you that had to be separated to facilitate your moving forward. Runners who in every instance have moved directly into a course of action put an invisible goal into a visible achievement. God has shared this same possibility with us through dreams, which allows moving the invisible into the visible mode. The realistic point to this is not everyone will appreciate your dreams and visions as in Joseph's case: **Genesis 37:5 (KJV)** *[5]And Joseph dreamed a dream, and he told it his brethren: and they hated him yet the more.* Do not allow their negative reactions to begin to imprison you because your goal is to recognize and eliminate those bars created over the years.

Therefore, God propelled your spirit into a miraculous season of possibilities where there is healing, help, and favor. But what is so special about you? Well, remember that Jesus Himself has taken an interest in you, and we call it favor.

In Hebrew, the word **"favor"** means to gaze steadily with interest or to regard with benevolence, which is kindness and compassion. This word never refers to a casual or disinterested glance. When God grants someone **His favor**, He takes a keen and lively interest in that person. He observes, watches, studies, and lovingly fixes His steady gaze on the one so favored. What an amazing privilege! So then, the favor of God is when God fixes His gaze upon you, even the details of your life.

He watches you walk. Return to the story of the Samaritan woman. She came to the well to draw water. The gaze of Jesus was upon her as she continued to walk in the midst of her many dilemmas. Her journey brought to mind the question found in *James 5:13(KJV) is any among you afflicted*.

An affliction carries symptoms: **hardship, misery, misfortune, distress, and weakness**. This affliction is also enfeebling and debilitating. It causes the body's physical or mental state to suffer. This state carries depression; there have always been lay-offs, foreclosures, repossessions, and un-employment. Businesses have closed their doors throughout time, and prison populations have increased. Credit card abuse still causes debts to soar to incredible levels as many end up in default or charge off. Many are struggling to keep lights on and food on the table. Yet, there is declining attendance in many churches or at the well. The world has caused the saints to reiterate their terminology and echo the word bailout. We should be sounding God's word, and He's saying Bail-in.

Deut 7:6 (KJV) ⁶For thou art an holy people unto the LORD thy God: the LORD thy God hath chosen thee to be a special people unto himself, above all people that are upon the face of the earth.

God is saying there is a condition in this process being overlooked. If you have not been, come in! If you have been away, come back! If you have been looking down, look-up! *Psalms121:1 (KJV) "I will lift up my eyes unto the hills, from whence cometh my help"*

The concept of stimulus has over shadowed God's conveyance to stimulate my people. Consider what has hindered the pursuit of your spirit. God says we are afflicted, but the good news is God has the cure for any and all affections!

2 Cor 4:17 (KJV) [17] *For our light affliction, which is but for a moment, worketh for us a far more exceeding and eternal weight of glory;*

Do not hang your head or disguise your joy. God is not a man that He should, would, could or will lie. Understand that He made you a promise that He would never leave you nor forsake you! Many people have the pictures, posters, and cards of the poem "Footprints" to remember that. God promised me and that is enough! People of God know any affliction that you are dealing with, the Lord knows! The Samaritan woman heading towards the well was afflicted. Jesus saw this woman's condition, and the scriptures disclose that Jesus started the conversation just as He does with us every morning. I have heard those exclaim, "You didn't have to wake me this morning Lord but you did." He whispered your name! In response, thank Him. What we look at is the natural; your clock did not save you this morning, are any among you afflicted?

Jesus offered the woman a cure! He gave her a prescription to fill and she was able to share with many today that which will heal, help, and release favor. *John 4:23 – 24 (KJV) ²³But the hour cometh, and now is, when the true worshippers shall worship the Father in spirit and in truth: for the Father seeketh such to worship him. ²⁴God is a Spirit: and they that worship him must worship him in spirit and in truth.*

The truth of the spirit is once you fill the prescription, the cure becomes more apparent; you begin to catch up with your spirit. Not many would see the help and favor in disguise. The happiness from this life test is truly the results of a promise. The afflictions that required the healing came from God himself.

In affliction there's

Deliverance:
Many who have presumed the worst outcome in every situation cannot see the reason why they did not get the job as a blessing. The

willingness to be absent from the body ideally and absent from worship may be the reasons God denied you the opportunity to work every other weekend. *Psalms 34:19 (KJV)* *[19]* *Many are the afflictions of the righteous: but the LORD delivereth him out of them all.*

Comfort of Gods presence:

Often we have worked ourselves to the point of exhaustion in order to get the wanted things and not needed things. Our body begins to suffer from neglect, and a temporary sickness forces you to rest. Now you can be in Gods presence, and He can minister to you *Isaiah 43:2 (KJV)* *[2]When thou passest through the waters, I will be with thee; and through the rivers, they shall not overflow thee: when thou walkest through the fire, thou shalt not be burned; neither shall the flame kindle upon thee.*

Membership in the company of the redeemed:

When you are among them, you have recovered from a similar situation. Healed from sickness or loss of fellowship there is no pointing of fingers. This is again revealed when those you love come to Christ. There are no accusations of them being counted less than yourself because you have the same likeness. *Revelation 7:13 (KJV)* *[13]And one of the elders answered, saying unto me, What are these which are arrayed in white robes? And whence came they?*

Sufficiency of divine grace:

Some people, by definition, have label success, achievements, and relationships as incapable or inaccessible because they have relied on your own concepts. *2 Corinthians 12:9 (KJV) ⁹And he said unto me, My grace is sufficient for thee: for my strength is made perfect in weakness. Most gladly therefore will I rather glory in my infirmities, that the power of Christ may rest upon me.*

His promises are and will be fulfilled. Whatever has afflicted you, your healing is here in your spirit. Catch up with your spirit God. has prepared a word to help instruct you through this troubled times. I didn't say "in" because we're coming through this thing. You are in the season of healing, help, and favor!

We must make mental preparation for the pursuit.

Romans 12:2 *"But be ye transformed by the renewing of your mind, that ye may prove what is that good, and acceptable, and perfect, will of God.*

No longer be overly involved by what we see or hear about others; the actions of others will cause us to suspend our apprehension of the spirit. Some people are unable to see because of damage to or defect in their eyes. Others, however, chose not to see, succumbing to egotism or self-righteousness, materialism, prejudice, greed, fear or even self-hate. Whatever the cause, the affliction of blindness can result.

Luke 18:40 – 43 (KJV) [40]And Jesus stood, and commanded him to be brought unto him: and when he was come near, he asked him, [41]Saying, What wilt thou that I shall do unto thee? And he said, Lord, that I may receive my sight. [42]And Jesus said unto him, Receive thy sight: thy faith hath saved thee. [43]And immediately he received his sight, and followed him, glorifying God: and all the people, when they saw it, gave praise unto God.

Bound from the starting block, and do your utmost because the spirit is so close it can almost be touched. Catch up with your spirit and receive your healing, help, and favor

In regard to **healing, help and favor** at some points we encounter what is considered a stain. The word stain refers to the worst of all situations and circumstances because a stain takes away from, soils, or taints. A stain brings ruin to whatever it touches, be it your new suit, dress or carpet. Once stained, the value is assumed lessened. What occurs when a life is considered stained, and what decisions should we face when trying to overcome the tainting or soiling?

Understand **"You're not where you are at this particular point in your life without reason."** Nothing that you've done so well or so right could have ever gotten you to this season of "the fulfillment of promises." Know beloved that it's because of **purpose, position, and destiny**.

God wanted to make known very clearly the unchangeable nature of His purpose so that we could fully understand His intentions.

God has positioned us I in the right place and situations, establishing us as heirs and joint heirs with Christ. His abundance renders us by name **"Children of the Promise"**

I fully understand that the word "promise" is an assurance that will or will not undertake a certain action or behavior, but, has potential for achievement and is afforded expectations. **This means you and I should be living in expectation that something is about to happen.**

The term **Children of the Promise** is spoken only **twice in the Bible:**

Romans 9:8(KJV) that is, they which are the children of the flesh, these are not the children of God: but the children of the promise are counted for the seed. Walking according to the Holy Spirit has caused a change in you.

Galatians 4:28(KJV) Now we, brethren, as Isaac was, are the children of promise. **You're not who you are by accident; you're of a promise.**

Heb 6:13 - 17 (KJV) [13]*For when God made promise to Abraham, because he could swear by no greater, he sware by himself,* [14]*Saying, Surely blessing I will bless thee, and multiplying I will multiply thee.* [15]*And so, after he had patiently endured, he obtained the promise.* [16]*For men verily swear by the greater: and an oath for confirmation is to them an end of all strife.* [17]*Wherein God, willing more abundantly to show unto the heirs of promise the immutability of his counsel, confirmed it by an oath:*

God confirmed His promise in an oath; **an oath is a solemn declaration** God made a commitment to a future action. In Hebrew, it's also defined as sacred restraint. That means to assign or consecrate, make holy or bless by divine spiritual influence, more so to control and confine or arrest situations or circumstances.

You are not where you are at this particular point in your life without reason! God had to place some things in your life under arrest! God had to start affecting the things you believe in so that you would believe more in Him. He started with your children, households, finances, and jobs.

He had to start affecting relationships where you thought people were turning their backs on you. He had to close doors and jobs because you were on time for work and late for church. You began to Miss Service after service because working tired you out.

When God moves on these things, it is easy to understand this statement **"If I don't have your M.I.N.D. (mind), you can't be M.I.N.E. (mine)!** God has purposed **healing, help and favor** the things you need. He has positioned you to **catch up with your spirit** right where you need to be.

As Children of Promise, you will reach your destiny, and His oath is a confirmation to end strife.

How do you know that you are purposed? If you go through a situation without stress, you are purposed. That means if you are laid off, out of work, or going through you still know He's:

JEHOVAH-JIREH

The name means, "Yahweh will provide" *Genesis 22:14(KJV) And Abraham called the name of that place Jehovahjireh: as it is said to this day, In the mount of the LORD it shall be seen*. This is the name given by Abraham in the scene of his offering up the ram, which was caught in the thicket on Mount Moriah. The expression is the equivalent of the saying, "Man's extremity is God's opportunity."

YOU ARE PURPOSED!

When people and circumstances around you are falling apart, and you are as cool as the Hebrew boys are in the fiery furnace, God becomes

JEHOVAH-NISSI

Jehovah my banner is the title given by Moses at the altar which he erected on the hill at the top of which he stood with uplifted hands while Israel prevailed over their enemies, the Amalekites. *Exodus 17:15 (KJV)And Moses built an altar, and called the name of it Jehovah-nissi:*

The enemy declares, "I've finally broken them. See God, these your children are throwing their hands up. "But what you're exactly doing is saying, "Handle it God."

When others are declaring you have to be pushed into your destiny, disagree. Moses, leading the children through the Red Sea, did not push them; he led them and stood out front where they could see him!

What you have to understand is you have been hanging on to people who are not going anywhere. Frequently, people hang on to you because you are supposed to lead them out.

If you understand that the Devil will push you while God will lead you, it becomes easier to reach your destiny. There is a challenge in reaching your destiny because some times things and people might be left behind.

Genesis 12:1-2 (KJV) *¹Now the LORD had said unto Abram, Get thee out of thy country, and from thy kindred, and from thy father's house, unto a land that I will show thee: ²And I will make of thee a great nation, and I will bless thee, and make thy name great; and thou shalt be a blessing:*
You have to display an understanding of Gods word and have patience; Abraham was ninety when the promise came and one hundred when it was fulfilled.

We became children of the promise by God's word to Abraham.

Genesis 22:17-18 (KJV) That in blessing I will bless thee, and in multiplying I will multiply thy seed as the stars of the heaven, and as the sand which is upon the sea shore; and thy seed shall possess the gate of his enemies; ¹⁸And in thy seed shall all the nations of the earth be blessed; because thou hast obeyed my voice. Other translations record: "They will conquer their enemies" (NLT) and "Your descendants will take possession of the cities of their enemies" (NIV)

In any translation you will receive happiness, peace, prosperity, and good things of every kind because God promised, and it is your destiny. If you have not reached your destiny, you are on your way. As you begin to receive the guidance of Holy Spirits, the word's intersection and re-section will affect your spirit. In the natural, an intersection is a mathematical term meaning to find a connecting position by starting from known points.

The term re-sections is to take a known place of reference and retrace your information to its beginning. In other words, to find my intersection I know I made some mistakes, and I have not done everything right. But God has allowed me through His revealing grace to make it another day.

When considering re-section, you need to really say with thought, "When I think of the goodness of Jesus and all He's done for me, I thank God for saving me." You have been brought into a season of fullness (healing) and fulfillment (help) of promises (favor), and God swore by Himself that He would.

Your coming out is a matter of being led by the Holy Spirit and knowing that because you're a seed, you are a child of promise. God has purposed you and positioned you, and your Destiny has been promised. Start speaking those things that are not as though they are. Take back the cities and secure the gates. Stand on the promise because God can, and He will.

Because the natural eye of man can only see what we present ourselves to be, many have become accomplished actors and great imitators. We must now ensure the receiving of our mantle handed down from generations to not only impress but also impact the lives of those around us. It doesn't become a matter of color, gender, status, or style; it's time for the healing to occur in the lives of those left bitter. It's time for the reaching out and back if necessary and pull those forward who have slipped or been left behind. Now is the time we affect a generation with the intense glare of favor because where God has destined me to go no man can deny my purpose, position or destiny. I've been especially trained for this day and time, and those who have observed my training know I am well prepared for my mission. God has sent me to engage an adversary whose main assignment was to deter me from reaching my destiny and to undermine my purpose. The comments and stereotypes of society were to afflict, but God positioned me not to fail, and victory is within reach. I have only to pursue for as David in *1 Samuel 30:8 And David inquired at the LORD, saying, Shall I pursue after this troop? shall I overtake them? And he answered him, Pursue: for thou shalt surely overtake them, and without fail recover all.* I, too, will inquire of the Lord, "Shall I pursue?" and His answer is "Pursue."

Chapter 3

Identified by your number!

~I am to become more than a reflection in a mirror.
I am to become a reflection of light to my children and a
beacon of hope to my children's-children~

Society has a system which provides identification. This system, with the aid of numbers, records your history from birth to death i.e. date of birth, social security number, student ID, drivers license and even birth order in a family. In the event of a crowd, we stay in line waiting until our number is called. In our earliest memory among others life lessons, we learned to count. The world as we see it today is experiencing crisis after crisis. These occurrences are not strange as the bible tells us these and other calamities will happen and to whom they will affect, the impenitent and unbelieving.

In truth, the tactics the enemy has chosen to employ have caused our focus to shift to that of doubt with the principle of "never enough" leading the way. This circumstance has also caused many to have no faith in today's economic system, but we can find assurance through Christ Jesus that God will and does still answer prayers. The promise we seek through blessings, the ones that desire to overtake us, must be given equal advantage to catch us. Therefore, God, because we are special to Him, employs various tactics because not all afflictions come from the enemy. *Isaiah 45:7* (**KJV**) says: *⁷I form the light, and create darkness: I make peace, and create evil: I the LORD do all these things.*

God's principal establishes us as those of highest importance to Him. Remember, the enemy knows the effects of a restored Spirit as well as God and is given far too much credit for our afflictions. **Psalms 34:19** (KJV) *Many are the afflictions of the righteous: but the LORD delivereth him out of them all.*

Remember, there is the power of authority versus position, what God has empowered you to do versus what the world has established. *Romans 8:35-39(KJV)* *³⁵Who shall separate us from the love of Christ? shall tribulation, or distress, or persecution, or famine, or nakedness, or peril, or sword? ³⁶As it is written, For thy sake we are killed all the day long; we are accounted as sheep for the slaughter. ³⁷Nay, in all these things we are more than conquerors through him that loved us. ³⁸For I am persuaded, that neither death, nor life, nor angels, nor principalities, nor powers, nor things present, nor things to come, ³⁹Nor height, nor depth, nor any other creature, shall be able to separate us from the love of God, which is in Christ Jesus our Lord.*

When we hear of reports of large companies struggling, we are reminded of time as it refers to the relationship of events within creation where each event moves linearly toward a future goal. The connection between God and time is that time itself has a reaction, which brings about a collapse, but God is timeless and He who created time stands above its flow. The word references such time: **Genesis 1:1 - 3 (KJV)** *¹In the beginning God created the heaven and the earth. ²And the earth was without form, and void; and darkness was upon the face of the deep. And the Spirit of God moved upon the face of the waters. ³And God said, Let there be light: and there was light.*

These words, the words God spoke, were and must be accomplished. Jesus has given us the same authority to create through his word regardless of whatever collapses around us. **John 14:13** *¹³And whatsoever ye shall ask in my name, that will I do, that the Father may be glorified in the Son. ¹⁴If ye shall ask any thing in my name, I will do it.*

In your day-to-day walk, you can turn to the power of God's word and begin speaking, not naming and claiming or blabbing and grabbing, but speaking the word of God that declares, "I am more than a conqueror." There is someone who is wondering today, "What is it about me?" Have you thought about yourself in the midst of these wide-ranging crises? Do you know what God can and will do for you and why?

God's word provides instructions that inspire faith in what He has promised. In fact, we must begin now to develop the living faith that will see us through these tricks and trials of life because the enemy knows even when we sometimes forget. **There is something about you!**

Have you ever had the occasion to meet a person who you believe you've met before or had someone walk up to you and ask, "Don't I know you."

Some people call it dé jà vu: *the illusion of remembering scenes and events when experienced for the first time: a feeling that one has seen or heard something or someone before.* When you cannot recall or believe its mistaken identity. Do you walk away racking your brain trying to figure out what was it about that person? They maybe asking themselves about you, almost puzzled. We say things such as, "I cannot put my finger on it. Who are your relatives? I know there is something about you! If I look long enough, maybe it will come to me! It might be I owe you something or you owe me something!" It is as if your spirit has moved them to proclaim, "I know there's something about you! Maybe I need to know you! Maybe we are related! Maybe you have been through something! Maybe you are coming out of something! Nevertheless, there is something about you!"

The Bible declares in
Psalms 139:14 (KJV) [14] *I will praise thee; for I am fearfully and wonderfully made: marvellous are thy works; and that my soul knoweth right well.* **So God didn't make any useless items,** I know this! Nevertheless, there's something about you!

Genesis 1:26 (KJV) [26]*And God said, Let us make man in our image, after our likeness: and let them have dominion over the fish of the sea, and over the fowl of the air, and over the cattle, and over all the earth, and over every creeping thing that creepeth upon the earth.*

You look like daddy, yet there's something about you! There's a clue as to why; **there's something about you that people recognize.**

In Deut 7:6-9 (KJV) [6]*For thou art an holy people unto the LORD thy God: the LORD thy God hath*

*chosen thee to be a special people unto himself,
above all people that are upon the face of the
earth. ⁷The LORD did not set his love upon you,
nor choose you, because ye were more in number
than any people; for ye were the fewest of all
people: ⁸But because the LORD loved you, and
because he would keep the oath which he had
sworn unto your fathers, hath the LORD brought
you out with a mighty hand, and redeemed you
out of the house of bondmen, from the hand of
Pharaoh king of Egypt. ⁹Know therefore that the
LORD thy God, he is God, the faithful God, which
keepeth covenant and mercy with them that love
him and keep his commandments to a thousand
generations;*

The children of Israel were at the end of their
fortieth (40) year of wandering and were at this
particular time in Moab. Moses had gathered the
congregation for a word, yet other people were
watching. Isn't it fascinating how people will
watch you!

Moses and the children of Israel had jour-
neyed and undergone to this point numerous
transitions. They walked in shoes that did not
wear out and neither did their clothes.

Deuteronomy 7:6 (KJV) *⁶For thou art an holy
people unto the LORD thy God: the LORD thy
God hath chosen thee to be a special people unto*

himself, above all people that are upon the face of the earth.

From Genesis to today, the family of Jacob has grown to be called a people. Not only a people, but also God declares, **"For thou art an holy people."** In their history to this point, normally when the children of Israel had gathered, it was to murmur.

They were afraid of the unknown. If it's dark, we can easily be captured. *Genesis 14:12-13 (KJV) 12And they took Lot, Abram's brother's son, who dwelt in Sodom, and his goods, and departed. (v13)And there came one that had escaped, and told Abram the Hebrew.*

They wanted water. The desire to satisfy a thirst will not silence the lips but cause them to excitedly speak with bitter thoughts. *Exodus 15:23 (KJV) 23And when they came to Marah, they could not drink of the waters of Marah, for they were bitter: therefore the name of it was called Marah.*

They wanted food. We often remember how things of old were before we experienced the pleasing taste of the future. *Exodus 16:2-3 (KJV) 2And the whole congregation of the children of Israel murmured against Moses and Aaron in the wilderness: (v3) And the children of Israel said unto them, would to God we had died by the hand of the Lord in the land of Egypt,* *when we sat by the flesh pots, and when we did eat bread to the full;*

Paul declares, "In all things I am instructed both to be full and to be hungry." Moses gathered the congregation according to *Deut 1:3* :(KJV) *³And it came to pass in the fortieth year, in the eleventh month, on the first day of the month, that Moses spake unto the children of Israel, according unto all that the LORD had given him in commandment unto them;*

***The first day of the eleventh month"* is Shebat,** on the Hebrew calendar. Moses gathered everyone for a word from the Lord, for some good news, and we all like good news. You see, Moses had seen the transitions of the children of Israel which brought them to that point.

1. A transition to a New Generation will mean change.

Moses was addressing a congregation that had become a new generation of people. God spoke to the children of Israel because they were afraid. ***Deut 1:35(KJV)*** *"Surely there shall not one of these men of this evil generation shall see that good land, which I sware to give unto your fathers.*

Every member of that generation had died except for Joshua and Caleb, so they, after wandering forty years, were a new generation. God brought the children of Israel through. As they stood and heard Moses, I wonder how many thought of the things which held them back like many do during the service. Moses says God called them "Holy!"

Holy means exalted or worthy, devoted entirely to God or the work of God, having a divine quality. Are you Holy?

What bothered you last year that should be left behind because you are Holy? You shouldn't be affected by what happened in December. By making it into January, you made it. You're a new generation. I like to say it this way: **"You've out grown your problems and they don't fit you anymore."**

Moses was telling the children of Israel, "You are special, and God says so! He has called you His."

2. You've made a transition to a new possession.

Israel had been slaves in Egypt, and God sent Pharaoh a word, *Exodus 6: 10(KJV) And the Lord said to Moses, Go in, tell Pharaoh King of Egypt to let the people of Israel go,"* In other words "Let my people Go!"

Moses stood and declared, "God has chosen you children of Israel, to be His people, His children **because there's something about you."**

Some people still do not believe God sees all: *2 Chronicles 16:9 (KJV) ⁹For the eyes of the LORD run to and fro throughout the whole earth, to show himself strong in the behalf of them whose heart is perfect toward him.*

God saw the child-like ways of Israel, and He sees yours. In Hebrew, "children" or "child" has various meaning. There are four stages that suited some of us at various.

- **Na-pe yous** means infant behavior or simple minded, un-skilled. Those know and hear but won't yield.
- **Pais** is a child slave or Servant; those who have become processed but not learned.
- **Tik-to** is a child produced from a special seed and planted in good ground.
- **Hu-ios** is a child now called son, which is our destiny.

Moses was saying God saw the **Pais in you** when you were a slave, a servant in Egypt. God saw the **Nepios in you**, when you were being difficult, murmuring in the wilderness. God saw the **Tikto in you** and remembered you're from the seed of promise, the seed of Abraham. God saw the **Huios in you** as a son. God sees all that you're going through, and **there's something about you,** just like the children of Israel.

In the Bible from the Books of **Genesis to Deuteronomy** there had been ten **tribes.** As Moses began to speak, there are only seven spoken of. You see three were wiped out in wars or feuds with each other, and when you read the history of Israel, you'll find that others were wiped out also. **You have people watching you**, wanting to talk with you or talk about you, lying on you or about you. But you do not have to worry. If they are not for you, they will wipe each other out trying to watch you. You see, when you're **God's possession, your Huios stands out** because you are a son, and sons are a delight to the father.

3. Moses spoke of a transition to a new experience.

In Egypt, the children of Israel heard of the many gods of the Egyptians. They had seen God deliver them, and everything was a new experience. Could you just imagine walking at night led by a pillar of fire or during the day by a cloud? **Deut 6:4 Hear O Israel, the Lord Our God is one Lord,** Now, He has taken them as one people. The children of Israel were like most churches today. We are many families and church names, but we are still part of one body.

1 Corinthians 16:17 - 19 (KJV) *[17]I am glad of the coming of Stephanas and Fortunatus and Achaicus: for that which was lacking on your part they have supplied. [18]For they have refreshed my spirit and yours: therefore acknowledge ye them that are such. [19]The churches of Asia salute you. Aquila and Priscilla salute you much in the Lord, with the church that is in their house.*

"For we being many are one" It was a new experience watching God provide.

4. The last transition revealed is a new revelation of God, the revelation of His Love.

From Genesis to Numbers, the Love of God is never spoken of, but in Deuteronomy Chapter Seven, we see the words "His Love" Verse 9 says **"because of God's Love He keeps his covenant to a thousand generations."** That is Good news.

There is something about you! Not only you, but your children too. I heard it said this way, "What is in you is in your children, and they are still transitioning."

You should look at them and say what others are saying about you. There's something about you! When they're not acting right, they're transitioning. They are in the wilderness and still wandering because there's something about them. You already know there's something about you. God chose you when there were many others around you in your family and on your job. But He chose you because there's something about you. People will look at your life. God chose you, so you can affect others, not be infected by their ways. You see, the ones others are turning their backs on will turn to you.

There's something about you. God chose you to pray for the weak. People will come to you and pour their hearts out. There's something about you. God chose you to witness to the Lazarus generation, the Joshua generation to become the children of Promise because there's word in you, Gods word.

Psalms 12:6 (KJV) 6 The words of the LORD are pure words: as silver tried in a furnace of earth, purified seven times.

"The words of the Lord are pure and when you speak them, situations will change!

In addition, the Bible says it this way, **"People will look at you and call you blessed."**

Be reminded of the story told of a man who had to move two thousand (2000) sheep across an immense desert. On this particular day, he is weary from a long day's journey and decides to settle camp for the night.

After securing his sheep, he now begins to prepare a meal for himself when suddenly the piecing howl of a wolf shatters the night air. The shepherd, from experience, knows to immediately place more wood on his fire in hopes that the flames will keep the wolf at bay.

Suddenly, from the other side of his camp he hears more wolves howling, and again he places more wood on the fire. The number of wolves could not be determined by the howls as they become louder and grow closer. The Shepherd places more wood on the fire in his attempt to make as much light as possible.

As the Shepherd constantly turns his head in the bright light of the fire not knowing what to expect, he does know that if the wolves attack, his sheep will be scattered and maybe lost. Then in amazement, he notices that through the light there are four-thousand (4000) eyes focused on him in the midst of this situation.

In a time of trouble, where's your focus when the enemy comes? Is it on Jesus our Shepherd or towards the sounds of trouble? *James 1:2(KJV) says:*

²My brethren, count it all joy when ye fall into divers temptations;

There is something about you and because of your connection with God, you can bend but "not be broken by problems of the world. Keep your focus on the Lord.

The reflection that we see in the mirror during one crisis after another is that of victory. Know the eyes of our children are upon us. They are to receive the history and lessons we pass to them. The main principle should be that "We will transition into a generation with the power and authority.

Chapter 4

Learning the Course.

*~If the Wisdom of the Word is not shared,
then knowledge will be wasted and
the bridge of hope will never be crossed~*

There is a saying that when many speak it permits their lives to be hindered. When a man or woman says, "I'm a product of my environment," what does that really mean? For reasons of heredity and environment, everything we do is accounted for by cause. It does not mean that where you came from is where you must stay. The value of learning life's lessons will take us further then some ever imagine. God allows distress and deprives us of the lesser good of pleasure in order to guide us toward the greater good in obtaining a spiritual education. When the doctrine of sovereign immunity cannot stand as a barrier, what do you do when faced with a test? When we declare by example, "I'm living for the Lord" on what are your standards really built? ***Job 1:8-12 (KJV)*** *⁸And the LORD said unto Satan, Hast thou considered my servant Job, that there is none like him in the earth, a perfect and an upright man, one that feareth God, and escheweth evil? ⁹Then Satan answered the LORD, and said, Doth Job fear God for nought? ¹⁰Hast not thou made an hedge about him, and about his house, and about all that he hath on every side? thou hast blessed the work of his hands, and his substance is increased in the land. ¹¹But put forth thine hand now, and touch all that he hath, and he will curse thee to thy face. ¹²And the LORD said unto Satan, Behold, all that he hath is in thy power; only upon himself put not forth thine hand. So Satan went forth from the presence of the LORD.*

This shows us that God consented to Job's enduring not because Job lacked either love or the environment of a loving heritage but precisely out of love. This brings Job to the point of viewing the glimpse. Job ***42:5 (KJV)*** *⁵I have heard of thee by the hearing of the ear: but now mine eye seeth thee.* Job had to remove himself from the situation and experience the beauty of God's vision in us. Many times God's ability to act is blocked because we have failed to invite His presence into it. This takes the building of a special relationship one free from the ignorance of this world and built on the solid foundation God's word.

In this is a time of encouragement and to those who are seeking direction and even correction, a time of preparation. The process has begun, and we who will make it through until the end must be prepared to throw back the rope of hope to pull those through who are still struggling. When we look to what the Bible details as great accomplishments through enduring and find numerous occurrences which are noted in the second month of the year, there is a course we must endure.

Many should regard this period as a time of great expectancy, particularly the promise of rebuilding from the book of Ezra. This prophet was assigned the title of scribe. His journal details the provisions that God gives us in order to restore us to stand in our rightful places in His family and Kingdom.

In the Old Testament, the Spirit of the Lord was upon those selected as leaders rather than to all of God's people. When the Spirit came to an individual, He brought with Him one or more gifts, which equipped the individual to serve God. In the New Testament, the Spirit according to Paul becomes vital to the believer's relationship to God. It is an assurance to God's "Children of promise." The conditions which we build upon today are a result of the constant and persistent efforts of a journey down the path designed for the faithful. We are now called Remnant, Now, Joshua, or Promised. We must acknowledge our priestly heritage.

Ezra 3:8 (KJV) *⁸Now in the second year of their coming unto the house of God at Jerusalem, in the second month, began Zerubbabel the son of Shealtiel, and Jeshua the son of Jozadak, and the remnant of their brethren the priests and the Levites, and all they that were come out of the captivity unto Jerusalem; and appointed the Levites, from twenty years old and upward, to set forward the work of the house of the LORD.*

Its important to consider that in establishing construction or remodeling of a Spiritual relationship in and with the Father that whenever the building begins, the complications with arise,***Ezra 4:1 (KJV)*** *¹Now when the adversaries of Judah and Benjamin heard that the children of the captivity builded the temple unto the LORD God of Israel;*

When the Jews, some fifty thousand (50,000) of them, were permitted to return to Jerusalem, it was not done without preparation. It was, however, the beginning of their or your spiritual restoration and served two purposes.

It was important to them as a people. **II Chronicles 36:23 (KJV)***"Who is there among* *you of all his people? The Lord his God be with him, and let him go up"*. It granted them favor and fulfilled the promise of God's word.

Ezra *1:1* (KJV)"*Now in the first year of Cyrus king of Persia, that the word of the LORD by the mouth of Jeremiah might be fulfilled, the LORD stirred up the spirit of Cyrus king of Persia,* He made a proclamation throughout all his kingdom and also put it in writing.

What applied to them in the year 536 BC also applies to us and Restoration is promised, but it will not be easy. We have to offer ourselves as a living sacrifice before God and continually pray. It is obvious from the state of the economy and the text that the enemy of God's people despises them and the church as much then as he does now. However, have faith, because God's people now as they did then know and believe in God's word. He knows me and has placed His name upon me.

Jeremiah 1:5 (KJV) Before I formed thee in the belly I knew thee; and before thou camest forth out of the womb I sanctified thee and I ordained thee a prophet unto the nations

My father will overthrow any enemy who attempts to destroy me. It is in His Word. We must learn to use God's word. Jesus was tempted by the devil.

Matthew 4:1 – 11 (KJV) *And when the tempter came to him, he said, If thou be the Son of God, command that these stones be made bread.* *⁴But he answered and said, It is written, Man shall not live by bread alone, but by every word that proceedeth out of the mouth of God.*
⁶And saith unto him, If thou be the Son of God, cast thyself down: for it is written, He shall give his angels charge concerning thee: and in their hands they shall bear thee up, lest at any time thou dash thy foot against a stone. ⁷Jesus said unto him, It is written again, Thou shalt not tempt the Lord thy God.⁹And saith unto him, All these things will I give thee, if thou wilt fall down and worship me. ¹⁰Then saith Jesus unto him, Get thee hence, Satan: for it is written, Thou shalt worship the Lord thy God, and him only shalt thou serve. ¹¹Then the devil leaveth him, and, behold, angels came and ministered unto him.

God cares for us continually. His abundant provision is with us in everything we undertake. Whatever we need is given to us daily and without fail. The body of Christ is growing with people facing issues they feel they cannot handle. They are coming. The homeless, hungry and helpless are coming; the neglected, abused and abandoned are coming.

Isaiah 29:8 KJV) *[8]It shall even be as when an hungry man dreameth, and, behold, he eateth; but he awaketh, and his soul is empty: or as when a thirsty man dreameth, and, behold, he drinketh; but he awaketh, and, behold, he is faint, and his soul hath appetite: so shall the multitude of all the nations be, that fight against mount Zion.*

They have been dreaming of abundance, yet sleep walking through life only to awaken still without evidence.

People are coming, seeking advise, direction and solutions. They are coming with lives that lay in ashes and ruin, yet they survived disaster to make it to the house of God to regenerate their spirits. **Ezekiel 34:29 (KJV)** *[29]And I will raise up for them a plant of renown, and they shall be no more consumed with hunger in the land, neither bear the shame of the heathen any more.*

These are "THE REMNANT PEOPLE" who endured for such a time as this because what they're going through and what we're going through was designed by God to encourage us and let us know

"GREAT THINGS ARE PROMISED TO US."

God had to show us that in order to rebuild, something first has to be torn down or taken away. **Jobs were taken away and the banking system torn down.** There has to be heartache and heartbreak to really know sorrow and cause the type of wailing that gets God's attention. So, the husband or the wife left, **but they we not suppose to be there anyway.** Nevertheless, in the midst of it all, you are on the right track towards restoration and rebuilding.

When your past was, based on a lifestyle of worldly ways, what you envisioned as success was not God's plan for you. *Isaiah 49:10 (KJV) They shall not hunger nor thirst; neither shall the heat nor sun smite them: for he that hath mercy on them shall lead them, even by the springs of water shall he guide them.*

In order to gain this new spiritual education, you couldn't out-think God.

Jeremiah 29:11 (KJV) ¹¹For I know the thoughts that I think toward you, saith the LORD, thoughts of peace, and not of evil, to give you an expected end.

Now in this period of rebuilding or establishing a foundation, build on FAITH, knowing the Lord's eyes are always watching over you. His power and presence are with you to overcome any obstacle you may face. Faith will begin to turn situations around. **WHEN YOU BUILD IT, THEY WILL COME!**

Ezra 4:1 (KJV) ¹Now when the adversaries of Judah and Benjamin heard that the children of the captivity builded the temple unto the LORD God of Israel; So like the Jews in the book of Ezra, the adversaries, the opposition to building will come your way, and they're coming with the determination to make you fail. They'll attack your mind, body and spirit when they think you're the weakness, but never think of yourself as being anything less than a child of God.

Job 13:15 (KJV) ¹⁵Though he slay me, yet will I trust in him:

Adversaries will approach the leadership, much like Zerubbal and Jeshua. However, God has given the anointing of wisdom to those who lead you, and if you continually build, you will prosper under the direction of His prophets. **Jesus told Peter the enemy will come:** *Luke 22:31 – 32 (KJV) ³¹And the Lord said, Simon, Simon, behold, Satan hath desired to have you, that he may sift you as wheat: ³²But I have prayed for thee, that thy faith fail not: and when thou art converted, strengthen thy brethren.*

They won't give up because if they can't discourage you or make you fearful, they will enlist the aid of others. **Ezra 4:5 (KJV)** *⁵And hired* *thirty-five () counselors against them, to frustrate their purpose,*

Nevertheless, No weapon that is fashioned against you shall prosper.

When you can sing with joy from your heart, your Hope is built on nothing less than Jesus Christ like as in ***Ezra 3:11 (KJV)*** *[11]And they sang together by course in praising and giving thanks unto the LORD; because he is good, for his mercy endureth for ever toward Israel. And all the people shouted with a great shout, when they praised the LORD, because the foundation of the house of the LORD was laid.*

Paul takes the opportunity to explain the responsibilities of Christians to the Thessalonians. He declares that when a message of the Gospel is empowered by the Holy Spirit, then that word enables those who have the spirit to respond positively. The opposite applies to those without the spirit's power. For them the Gospel is merely words.

1 Thessalonians 5:14 - 24 (KJV) *[14]Now we exhort you, brethren, warn them that are unruly, comfort the feebleminded, support the weak, be patient toward all men. [15]See that none render evil for evil unto any man; but ever follow that which is good, both among yourselves, and to all men. [16]Rejoice evermore. [17]Pray without ceasing. [18]In every thing give thanks: for this is*

*the will of God in Christ Jesus concerning you.
[19]Quench not the Spirit. [20]Despise not proph-
esyings. [21]Prove all things; hold fast that which
is good. [22]Abstain from all appearance of evil.
[23]And the very God of peace sanctify you wholly;
and I pray God your whole spirit and soul and
body be preserved blameless unto the coming of
our Lord Jesus Christ. [24]Faithful is he that cal-
leth you, who also will do it.*

If the world does not see Jesus in His people,
it is not likely to look for Him anywhere else. If
we ask, "why Lord?" when we're going through,
why not ask "why Lord?" when we've made it
out?

Paul uses these exhortations in dealing with
attitudes of believers as individuals regarding
their lives before God and knowing their duties

1. Personal Living

Among the living everyday is the most over
looked blessing of all. Many go to bed with the
expectation that tomorrow will come. When God
calls us to another day, how real is the statement
"This is the day that the Lord has made, I will
rejoice and be glad in it?" God wants His people
to be joyful, and He gives them every reason to
be. Nevertheless, Paul knew human nature well

enough to sense the need for a reminder to rejoice at all times.

2. Corporate Living

Whereas individual responsibility in personal behavior is expected, corporate living deals with life in the assembly of believers. We all have the responsibility and ability to do this though some have more discernment than others. Among the assembled saints, treating others as you expect to be treated is of great importance. However, how you treat them when you're not among the assembly matters more. What is revealed in following the Word should be retained, and a key principle in corporate living.

3. Divine Enablement

In divine enablement Paul, expressed his religious wish that God would enable all to attain it. We are not by God's will for our lives to struggle. The Lord becomes the immovable on which we rest, and it is on His word we stand. He is not good to me only some of the time; He is good to me all of the time. His love for me endures forever, and we have a right to praise Him. Moreover, when the foundation is finished, we build in surety. That is Divine Enablement.

How's your foundation? When the restoration and building begin, remember just what God did for you in the past, He will do in the future, the Lord has provided deliverance for you in every area of your life. He does not desire for any of His children to be in bondage in any way. You are free in Christ Jesus. If you do not know Him, it's time. Study to show yourself approved unto the Lord; learn to observe His ways and begin to know your place in Kingdom living. Spiritual pursuit in this time leads to the keys called: **RESTORATION** and **EXPECTANCY!** In addition, they come with responsibilities. Our responsibilities include building others with words that inspire. When others come with words such as "IF" and "Maybe," which we think are encouragements, they speak in order to break your concentration. Remember, they may interrupt your concentration for a moment but will never be able to break your connection. Your spirit is your connection to God, and the course you take was especially selected for you.

Chapter 5

The Commitment to Finish

*~If I continue to trust in Him, then He will
continue to lead, for where He
led me, I would have never made
it on my own~*

If ever the word "choose" played any part in your future, you now have reached the point of restoration and expectancy. You now have to make a decision. Do you stay on or do you jump off? Generally, any system of thought that attempts to define the nature of something is composed of two distinct realities: substances (what I can see) or principles (what I use to obtain what I see). To see the finish line ahead is far different than to know it is around the corner.

The commitment of this pursuit is about to cause a shift in your household and way of living if it has not already. It is by the abundant blessings of the Lord that increase will come and your substances **will be multiplied**. In describing the nature of reality, if you have been sharing the ideas and teaching of this book and its principals, **eyebrows are being raised** as well as thoughts. I can tell you that plots are being formed to deter your pursuit. There is now a distinction between the physical and the spiritual, between the invisible and the visible, and between matter and mind.

The prophet Ezekiel had a congregation called Israel, which often refused to listen to God. The vision to see as a church and as the body was what God was telling and showing Ezekiel about navigating the waters of a spirit filled life. What we now see happening in the church has caused some to become hesitant about their walk with Jesus. Some fear that God may require more of us than we are willing to give. We reason within ourselves that, if we do not commit to the work fully, then we will not be found guilty of failing in our commitment to Christ.

Think on these three questions before going further.

1. Are you living in the center of God's perfect will in your life?
2. Have you reached a level of spiritual maturity and obedience to God's word that you feel God wants you to have?

3. When it comes to walking according to the word of God, where are you?

Ezekiel 47:1-3 (NIV)(1)Then the man brought me back to the entrance of the temple. There I saw a stream flowing eastward from beneath the temple threshold. This stream then passed to the right of the altar on its south side. (2) The man brought me outside the wall through the north gateway and led me around to the eastern entrance. There I could see the stream flowing out through the south side of the east gateway. (3) Measuring as he went, he led me along the stream for 1,750 feet and told me to go across. At that point the water was up to my ankles. (4) He measured off another 1,750 feet and told me to go across again. This time the water was up to my knees. After another 1,750 feet, it was up to my waist. (5) Then he measured another 1,750 feet, and the river was too deep to cross without swimming. (6a) He told me to keep in mind what I had seen:

Remember if it's not in God word, it's a lie. It comes from the enemy (Satan), and he is a liar who spreads lies to create further obstacles. In Chapters Thirty-eight (38) and Thirty-nine (39), Ezekiel dealt with a spirit which caused doubt among people. God had Ezekiel to prophesy against Gog, the prince of Meshech and Tubal *Ezekiel 39:1(KJV) "Therefore, thou son of man prophesy against Gog and say, thus saith the Lord God: Behold I am against thee;*

God's judgment was upon Gog, who was seeking control, causing carnal security among the people (they were secure in doing wrong) and polluting the land with lies or as the Bible says "Evil Attempts." God reserved a place just for him and his followers: *Ezekiel 39: 11* (KJV)*And it shall come to pass in that day, that I will give unto Gog a place there of graves in Israel, the valley of the passengers on the east of the sea: and it shall stop the noses of the passengers: and there shall they bury Gog and all his multitude: and they shall call it The valley of Hamongog.*

Ha-mon-gog means a warm place.

After making the people of Israel victorious, God then made preparations for them to receive their inheritance and finally instructions for the temple: "Don't leave the way you came." *Ezekiel 46:9 (KJV)But when the people of the land shall come before the LORD in the solemn feasts, he that entereth in by the way of the north gate to worship shall go out by the way of the south gate; and he that entereth by the way of the south gate shall go forth by the way of the north gate: he shall not return by the way of the gate whereby he came in, but shall go forth over against it.*

God allowed Ezekiel to see the water as it flowed from the temple and became a mighty river that brought life, healing, and deliverance to a dry and thirsty land.

This land was the inheritance, the home of God's chosen people, Israel. Likewise, God has great things in store for us who are heirs and joint heirs with Christ! **We, like Ezekiel, are allowed to see the water and our inheritance**, but the Jezebel spirit which seeks the spiritual inheritance of you and those connected to you has caused some to doubt. When Ezekiel first saw the waters, he could not and did not go into the water alone.

There are many who hear the Gospel and see what the spirit can and is doing in the lives of others, yet that is as far as they get! They never really get in the water! Why? It is because they are watching you!

When the Holy Spirit deals with the life of a sinner, that sinner must respond either in **Repentance** or **Rebellion.** If our response is one of repentance, then God saves us and we begin the journey through life with Him. If our response is rebellion then Hamon Gog (the warm place) will be your destiny. **(Remember they are watching)**

What God showed Ezekiel then allows us to examine ourselves today. God's people have access to the water and answer the question?

"How deep are you in this?" *Ezekiel 47: 3(NIV) Measuring as he went, he led me along the stream for 1,750 feet and told me to go across. At this point the water was up to my ankles.*

Ankle Deep

Romans 10:9(KJV) if thou shalt confess with thy mouth the Lord Jesus and shalt believe in thine heart that God hath raised him from the dead, thou shalt be saved. Once we confess, we gain access.

At this point, we begin our walk with the Lord.

Water has long presented a problem for men. Many times, we just check it out first, kick our shoes off or roll up our pants because ankle deep is fine for young Christians. But soon, older ones hang out here too!
There are several explanations for this behavior:

1. Some still behave the way they want to.
This is the very moment where those who seek direction become misguided. This is why the pursuit you undertake must be fully understood. When the word is empowered by the Holy Spirit, then that word enables those who have the spirit to respond positively.

2. Some refuse correction.

This is the opposite effect of the word "being." Those without the spirit's power find that the Gospel is merely words and when the pursuit begins and their direction is without reason, they will not accept directions back to the right road. They would rather travel aimlessly than accept the fact they were wrong.

3. Some behave according to their own thinking.

The Holy Spirit warms the heart, enlightens the mind, and empowers people's spirit. Paul warned against hindering its fire, which can be snuffed out if resisted.

4. There is very little resistance to changing direction.

The Lord cannot order their steps because they have not yet learned to recognize the Voice of God.

Remember, Ankle-Deep is the point where they first find forgiveness, but it's also where the toughest battles are fought. God still gently wants to lead them into a deeper relationship, but they have to stay in the water because someone is watching!

Ezekiel 47:4a (KJV) He measured off another 1,750 feet and told me to go across again. This time the water was up to my knees.

Knee Deep

1. **The walk becomes a little harder.**

   Individual responsibility and personal behavior create a disconnect and not being able to see the path becomes an excuse.

2. **Fear sets in (Aqua phobia or Hydro phobia).**

   The words Aqua phobia and Hydrophobia reflect the fear of water, and in spirit the water represents the word. The ability to receive and communicate direct revelations from the word of God may deter some with the fear that comes when these revelations concern future events or deal with the present.

3. **Things that can make you stumble are hidden.**

   The temptation to put the ideas of men on an equal footing with the word of God is still present.

Serving God in knee-deep water means that we must work a little harder, study a little more, do a little more, become more committed to what needs to be done and where we're suppose to be.

God will begin the process of strengthening your walk and building your faith in Him.

Ezekiel 47:4b (NIV) *after another 1,750 feet, it was up to my waist*

Waist Deep

1. Now the goings gets tougher because of the pull.

2. The demands of your time, energy, and commitment cut into your busy schedule.

God has now called you into training for leadership within His church. Now you have to read more, study more, pray harder and be concerned for a part of God's work that He has entrusted you with. When you are waist deep, here comes opposition:

1. Those who have not committed themselves will call you foolish for following those people.
2. They won't agree with your conviction or methods
3. They will even try to convince you that you cannot do what you feel God is telling you to do.

There will always be those who only venture ankle deep, or are toe testers or haven't even been in the water at all. They will try to discourage you from going farther for God.

Ezekiel 47:5(NIV) then he measured another 1,750 feet, and the river was too deep

Ezekiel was carried into water that was too deep for him to touch bottom and he had to swim. When you get committed to God to the point that you can't touch the bottom, that's the place where you must learn to depend upon the leading of Holy Spirit more than ever. You realize you can't do what God called you to do on your own. *Proverbs 3:6(KJV) in all thy ways acknowledge him and he shall direct thy paths* When you are this deep, you have gone beyond your ability.

Ezekiel had gone so far from shore that he could not walk back. Wherever the river flowed, that is where Ezekiel was going. The current was so strong and the volume of water so great that Ezekiel was in over his head. Still, God was carrying him, so there was no danger of the prophet drowning. God was still in control of the water and the life of the prophet. How deep are you in this?

Most Christians will never experience the joy, fulfillment, trust and love for God that comes with this kind of commitment because they love the safety of the shore too much. They refuse to leave their comfort zones. They refuse to stretch and grow beyond what they can see. Their faith is never exercised to the point that they have complete peace, no matter what the world throws at them.

True spiritual maturity is all about coming to the end of ourselves and realizing just how big God really is. God will not fail you. He is faithful and well able to take care of you. He is Jehovah-Jireh, the Lord that Provides. Walking in water that is only ankle deep requires little effort. The force of the water against your steps is minimal, and you can easily get in or out at will. It is also easy for some outside force such as wind or the push of a friend to knock you out of the water. Ankle-deep people accept Wind Doctrine when it blows their way. They do not know God's voice, so they listen to every little voice that makes them feel good or justifies their shallow walk. Walking in knee-deep water requires a little more effort, but it is still easy to be knocked out of the water by the same circumstances.

Jesus called those two kinds of people "lukewarm," and these are the ones who he will spew out of his mouth*. **Rev 3:16(KJV)** So then because thou art lukewarm, and neither cold nor hot, I will spue thee out of my mouth*

How deep are you in this? It is only those who will get at least waist deep or in over their heads in a deep commitment to Jesus who will ever really experience the glory of victory in Christ. What about you right now? Are you still in shallow water? What are you going to do with your commitment to the Lord? Will you surrender all or continue to walk in the shallow water? You're being watched. The choice is yours, and Jesus is waiting for your answer. Jesus will let you walk in deep water if you walk with Him. How deep are you in this? Consider the Latin term *assensus* which refers to the intellectual acquiesce to or acceptance of theological truth. The Biblical concept of faith is not guaranteed to be present without exercising saving faith in Christ. In pursuit of your spirit, how deep are you into your commitment?

Chapter 6

Race in spite of

~The plainly wrapped
gift is often the last one opened~

If you're determine now more than ever to continue, understand now how the problems you've been facing will be overcome. You're closer to the promise than ever before. The blessing that you have been receiving by now will fail in comparison to what is ahead as you adopt these furthering concepts. Could you imagine walking into a meeting where you knew that the people assembled didn't care for you, and their conversations about you consisted of comments questioning your heritage or birth rite? Would that deter your walk or cause you to dread going into such an event? Many who proclaim the Christian faith and those who have yet to accept Christ run or shy away from situations just like this. What do you do when circumstances are not as they appear? Examine one whose situation can attest to this theory, David.

1 Samuel 16:10-13 (KJV) [10]Again, Jesse made seven of his sons to pass before Samuel. And Samuel said unto Jesse, The LORD hath not chosen these. [11]And Samuel said unto Jesse, Are here all thy children? And he said, There remaineth yet the youngest, and, behold, he keepeth the sheep. And Samuel said unto Jesse, Send and fetch him: for we will not sit down till he come hither. [12]And he sent, and brought him in. Now he was ruddy, and withal of a beautiful countenance, and goodly to look to. And the LORD said, Arise, anoint him: for this is he. [13]Then Samuel took the horn of oil, and anointed him in the midst of his brethren: and the Spirit of the LORD came upon David from that day forward.

This event is rich with promises for the sons and daughters of God, who are called **"the children of promise."** They are still struggling to grasp the reality of today's troubles without the revelation of God's word, which is the same yesterday, today and forever. We are in a time where God is settling matters on our behalf, and from 1 Samuel it is made more evident in our seeking God for solutions. The children or Israel had asked of God a king and after ignoring His warnings, they repeated their request. God consented and Saul became King. After a period of trials for Saul, the Lord God in a moment of regret, speaks to Samuel

1 Sam 15:11 (KJV) *[11]It repenteth me that I have set up Saul to be king: for he is turned back from following me, and hath not performed my commandments.*

So enter the Shepherd boy David because God has a matter to settle on His people's behalf; *1 Sam 16:1 (KJV) fill thine horn with oil, and go, I will send thee to Jesse the Bethlehemite: for I have provided me a king among his sons.*

This lets us know the One in whom we have set our trust is well able to fulfill His word on our behalf. When we lose focus, we can and will stand and remain alert to the revelation of the Lord. He is ever ready to provide us with a vision for living. Moreover, while there are economical challenges ahead, we have a continuous reminder:

"It's not what it looks like."

David was in the position of servant and in servitude for various reasons. It did not bother him, how about you? David was ridiculed by his brothers and sent to tend sheep in the pasture with the servants where bears, lions and thieves dwelled.

1 Peter 5:8 (KJV) *⁸Be sober, be vigilant; because your adversary the devil, as a roaring lion, walketh about, seeking whom he may devour:*

John 10:10 (KJV) ¹⁰The thief cometh not, but for to steal, and to kill, and to destroy:

David went willingly and learned of God's providence for our lives because providence is being in God's protective care. **In fact, Jesus finishes the verse with** "I am come that they might have life, and that they might have it more abundantly. God's will, creates situations for us just as He did for David.

1. David's brothers got their father to agree and sent him out with the sheep. To add insult, they gave him a staff. **"It's not what it looks like!** It was their misfortune because the staff represents **AUTHORITY,** and this error put David in position as the Head.
2. They sent David to the pasture with the sheep, mistake number two.

David's father Jesse was rich and head herdsman in his tribe. His sheep were a major source of his riches, and the brothers sent David out as the head to watch over their **INHERITANCE**. **"It's not what it looks like!** David went out to the pasture ahead and not behind. Like David, all those who think they have put you out are actually putting you ahead.

In the pasture, David learned three ways to receive the promises of God:

Forgiving, Believing and Setting the atmosphere.

FORGIVENESS

Forgiving and being forgiven is walking in God's abundant mercy.
To obtain this promise of abundant mercy, you're going to have to forgive the very person or persons who may have never cared for you. David saw God as ever present and ever willing to help. He understood that God longed for fellowship and that the abundance of God's law was there for the purpose of guiding us to a fulfilling and joyful life, and not a means of bondage. In spite of how others treat me, God will provide.

Proverbs 25:21-22 (KJV)If thine enemy be hungry give him bread to eat; and if he be thirsty, give him water to drink (22) For thou shalt heap coals of fire upon his head, and the Lord shall reward thee

BELIEVING

Believing is faith in the power of the tongue by affirming your trust in the Lord Believe and speak your way into the God kind of life. Know that you are a favored one of God. He has set you apart as His ambassador. You are a part of the royal line. You are a child of the King and royalty speaks in decrees.

Deut 28:12 - 13 (KJV) *[12]The LORD shall open unto thee his good treasure, the heaven to give the rain unto thy land in his season, and to bless all the work of thine hand: and thou shalt lend unto many nations, and thou shalt not borrow. [13]And the LORD shall make thee the head, and not the tail; and thou shalt be above only, and thou shalt not be beneath;*

SETTING THE ATMOSPHERE

Praise and worship allow you to loosen yourself from the bonds of religious idealism and false dignity. Praise God freely with all of your heart, the way you know God wants you to. **Hosea 10:11** states "Judah *shall plow*"; which means break up, turn over, make right for seeding. Judah is your praise. You can go into enemy territory and cause the enemy to flee because when he thinks he's captured you, you can turn the table.

Acts 16:25 - 26 (KJV) *²⁵And at midnight Paul and Silas prayed, and sang praises unto God: and the prisoners heard them. ²⁶And suddenly there was a great earthquake, so that the foundations of the prison were shaken: and immediately all the doors were opened, and every one's bands were loosed.*

Following these steps lead to Kingdom living, and a focus on the Kingdom of God instead of the cares of this present world. When God and I get together for a heart-to-heart talk, He reveals to me hidden and unsearchable things that I could never discover on my own. David did not suffer in the pasture. When he was summoned to the house, he walked prophetically towards his destiny and spoke on the way of what he had learned of God.

Psalms 23:1-6 (KJV)

¹ The LORD is my shepherd; I shall not want. ² He maketh me to lie down in green pastures: he leadeth me beside the still waters. ³ He restoreth my soul: he leadeth me in the paths of righteousness for his name's sake. ⁴ Yea, though I walk through the valley of the shadow of death, I will fear no evil: for thou art with me; thy rod and thy staff they comfort me.

David arrives at the door someone is at his or her door today because right now the ears of God are tuned in to this prayer. The fulfillment of His promises are in your mouth Speak it! When David walked in, he didn't look like the king, but Samuel obeyed Gods word:

1 Sam 16:12 (KJV) *And the LORD said, Arise, anoint him: for this is he.*

You might not look like much in the natural, but in the spirit, you are victory marching. You are mighty in your walk, and the things of this world are subject to your words. When David was anointed, he did not brag or boast. He headed back to the presence of the Lord and finished his song;

5 Thou preparest a table before me in the presence of mine enemies: thou anointest my head with oil; my cup runneth over. 6 Surely goodness and mercy shall follow me all the days of my life: and I will dwell in the house of the LORD for ever.

It is often not what it looks like! You can and will go everywhere the Lord sends you and do whatever He commands you to do. You will not allow fear to hinder you in your calling. You know that God's power is within you wherever you go, and there is nothing which can overcome you. You have His word in your heart and in your mouth. You will speak it with purpose for an intended result because the faithful love that He promised to David has become your own.

After David's brothers witnessed his coronation, the importance of their role as his oppressors diminished. They were left in a temporary state of awe. It was temporary because the Bible later indicates their renewed attitude towards their brother. In fact, their testimony is much like many today who have seen the hand of God at work but have short-term memory.

They are the many who will not come to the house of God based on what they have heard or seen from the walk of the children of God during a time of panic.

If we, in fact, subscribe to this time of woe, it allows those same few to join the bandwagon and repeat worries. If we realize that it's not what it looks like and repeat it based on David's three lessons "forgive, believe and set the atmosphere," then we catch their attention. They begin to ask how can they get to where you are and say, they believe God is able. Then you have changed their perspective, and you guide those who were once blind. Now they see that no situation is hopeless.

They may be surrounded by despair but their help is near.

2 Kings 6:15-17 (KJV) [15]And when the servant of the man of God was risen early, and gone forth, behold, an host compassed the city both with horses and chariots. And his servant said unto him, Alas, my master! how shall we do? [16]And he answered, Fear not: for they that be with us are more than they that be with them. [17]And Elisha prayed, and said, LORD, I pray thee, open his eyes that he may see. And the LORD opened the eyes of the young man; and he saw: and, behold, the mountain was full of horses and chariots of fire round about Elisha.

Elisha, the prophet, asked his spiritual head Elijah for a double portion of his spirit. The prophet told him: **"If you see me when I'm taken up, (during my coronation), it will be yours."** Elisha saw Elijah taken into heaven by a whirlwind when the chariot appeared with horses of fire, and the two were separated accordingly.

2 Kings 2:9-11 (KJV) [9]And it came to pass, when they were gone over, that Elijah said unto Elisha, Ask what I shall do for thee, before I be taken away from thee. And Elisha said, I pray thee, let a double portion of thy spirit be upon me. [10]And he said, Thou hast asked a hard thing: neverthe-

less, if thou see me when I am taken from thee, it shall be so unto thee; but if not, it shall not be so. ¹¹*And it came to pass, as they still went on, and talked, that, behold, there appeared a chariot of fire, and horses of fire, and parted them both asunder; and Elijah went up by a whirlwind into heaven.*

When the two prophets witnessed the same miraculous feat, Elisha's request was established. Remember, it's not what it looks like! The revelation of this feat, which goes unnoticed, is **it was not because Elisha saw the fire, horses, whirlwind, and chariot in the natural, but rather because he had obtained the same spiritual insight that Elijah the prophet had.** He had received it and others saw a different of evidence to the fact.

2 Kings 2:15 (KJV) ¹⁵*And when the sons of the prophets which were to view at Jericho saw him, they said, The spirit of Elijah doth rest on Elisha. And they came to meet him, and bowed themselves to the ground before him.*

When the sons of the prophets, who *were* to view at Jericho saw him, they said, "The spirit of Elijah doth rest on Elisha." Moreover, they came to meet him and bowed themselves to the ground before him.

How is it that even today, there are those who will declare that they see the anointing that rests on your life, but miss the movement of God's spirit on a daily basis? Through periods of challenge, those who follow tremendously anointed men and women of God and still walk in misery and depression. They should be walking a proud and prophetical walk and be a wonderful presentation, a living vision of over-comers because it's God's will for our lives.

The test today for all who would hear on today and to every man and woman of God is to declare, **"I've become a servant of the Lord, and if you can use anybody Lord use me."** Elisha was in a place recorded as **Dothan,** which in biblical history has two significant points.

The first is the land of the twin wells, fertile and rich lands with layers of hills, which form a wave of various heights. The second point is this very place is recorded as where Joseph went to find his brothers who then sold him into slavery.

But in Dothan we find two more significant points: **Revelation, and Divine Presence.** The danger for Israel was apparent to Elisha's servant, but God's strength and presence were not. It was much like what we are faced with today. Nobody has to tell you about jobs, and money is far beyond acting funny. We are too frequently blinded by the seemingly overwhelming obstacles directly in front of the path to victory and cannot focus our sight on God's deliverance and presence just beyond the first horizon. Many a gospel hymn reminds us of God's goodness found early in the morning. How refreshing would you find it to sing these words in the morning light before the crisis arise?

I come to the Garden alone,
While the dew is still on the roses.
And the voice I hear, falling on my ear,
The son of God discloses.

And he walks with me and he talks with me,
And he tells me I am his own.
And the joy we share as we tarry there,
None other has ever known.

This is why early is so important. *1 Samuel 1:19(KJV) Early the next morning they arose and worshiped before the LORD and then went back to their home at Ramah. Elkanah lay with Hannah his wife, and the LORD remembered her.* Here Elkanah did not think, he just went this knowing his prayers could and would be answered in spite of the circumstances.

What do we ponder when opportunity arises to be in the Lords presence? *2 Chronicles 29:20(KJV)Early the next morning King Hezekiah gathered the city officials together and went up to the temple of the LORD.*

We are we in this condition because we fear the darkness, but we are light in this situation. *Mark 1:35(KJV) Very early in the morning, while it was still dark, Jesus got up, left the house and went off to a solitary place, where he prayed.*

There are times when our blessing stares us right in the face, and we miss it because it is too obvious. *John 21:4(KJV) Early in the morning, Jesus stood on the shore, but the disciples did not realize that it was Jesus.*

Elisha accustomed his servant to rise early. That is the way to bring something to pass and to do the work of a day in its day. On this day, the Servant ran straight to Elisha, and cried: *"Alas, master!" "What shall we do?* David was emboldened: **Psalms 3:6** [6] *I will not be afraid of ten thousands of people, that have set themselves* against me **Psalms 27:3** *Though an host should encamp against me, my heart shall not fear: though war should rise against me, in this will I be confident.*

We know the one in whom we have put our trust; we also know that there are many more who are on our side than in any army against us. Yet, are you blinded or frightened by what these financial experts are declaring shall be you escape route? The Lord is our shield *Psalms 33:20-22 (KJV)* [20] *Our soul waiteth for the LORD: he is our help and our shield.* [21] *For our heart shall rejoice in him, because we have trusted in his holy name.* [22] *Let thy mercy, O LORD, be upon us, according as we hope in thee.*

What Elisha said to his servant is spoken to all the faithful servants of God when without is strife and within are fears*: Romans 8:31(KJV).* [31]*What shall we then say to these things? If God be for us, who can be against us?* We are not afraid when the enemy comes in like a flood. However, the enemy may come in the night and surround us with a great host. We are not stirred to terror when others panic and cry out in fear. Instead, we will remain steadfast, for God will fight our battles.

Exodus 14:14 (KJV) [14]*The LORD shall fight for you, and ye shall hold your peace.*

2 Samuel 5:24 (KJV) [24]*And let it be, when thou hearest the sound of a going in the tops of the mulberry trees, that then thou shalt bestir thyself: for then shall the LORD go out before thee, to smite the host of the Philistines.*

Elisha stood upon the hilltop in Dothan and saw himself safe. Many stand on the same faith that says, "I do not trust in what I see, for I know that what I do not see is where the real power is. "The Lords angels have surrounded us to do battle on our behalf. Therefore, we cannot and will not be shaken, and we will not be afraid.

Elisha wished no more than our will for today; his prayer was that his servant might see. I pray for every believer "Lord Give them sight." **The sight I speak of is Spiritual vision. Spiritual vision prepares you for afflictions: Job 42:5 (KJV)** *⁵I have heard of thee by the hearing of the ear: but now mine eye seeth thee.*

Spiritual vision is purely essential to your heart: **Matt 5:8 (KJV)** *⁸Blessed are the pure in heart: for they shall see God. The Holy Spirit is the author of Spiritual vision: John 16:14 - 15 (KJV) ¹⁴He shall glorify me: for he shall receive of mine, and shall show it unto you. ¹⁵All things that the Father hath are mine: therefore said I, that he shall take of mine, and shall show it unto you.*

Believers alone possess Spiritual vision: **John 14:19 (KJV)** *¹⁹Yet a little while, and the world seeth me no more; but ye see me: because I live, ye shall live also. Spiritual vision causes you to have a telescope of faith:*

Heb 11:27 (KJV) *²⁷By faith he forsook Egypt, not fearing the wrath of the king: for he endured, as seeing him who is invisible?* The opening of our eyes will be the silencing of our fears. In the dark, we are most apt to be frightened. The clearer the sight we have of the sovereignty and power of heaven the less will fear the calamities of this earth.

You are standing atop Dothan or on the hill with the sheep. God had to put us in a position where we can now see clearly. Such was the case with Elisha's servant. The prophet never lost his Spiritual focus. The greatest kindness we can do for those who are fearful and faint-hearted is pray for them to be under the mighty grace of God. He will: GIVE THEM SIGHT to over take the promise and be overtaken by their blessings. We must continue the pursuit in spite of obstacles.

Chapter 7

Now I See....

*~The waves at the top of the waters often
hide the calm beneath the sea~*

These are those whose spirits would suffer a defeat because of blindness that is both Physical and Spiritual. In the midst of this blindness chaos reigns because they yield to worldly solutions. They suffer from wounds and abuse. Their afflictions, however temporary have caused them not to look for God only because they have not been educated to the cause of their blindness, whether physical or spiritual.

Physical causes of blindness could be from birth **John 9:1 (KJV)** *[1]And as Jesus passed by, he saw a man, which was blind from his birth.* Others causes include a developmental defect or infection. The body of man often seeks and, by many means, hinders the spirit. We hunger and thirst in the natural, and the effects can lead to a broken will or lost of birthright. In Genesis, upon returning from the chase and urged by the cravings of hunger, Esau sold his birthright to his brother, Jacob.

Spiritual blindness is a great human dilemma. The children of Israel were chosen to be God's servants. **Isaiah 42:19 (KJV)** *¹⁹Who is blind, but my servant? or deaf, as my messenger that I sent? Who is blind as he that is perfect, and blind as the LORD'S servant?* As a people, they were blind to their destiny. Consider this point; many of the spiritually blind do not know they are blind.

The servant of Elisha, who stood atop of Dothan along-side the watchman of his era, observed the enemy assembly and received sight. Today, many watchmen of God are still standing and have sounded **"the Shofar"** to alert the people of God and call them to a readiness to pray. However, this generation would rather watch a movie on mute and attempt to read lips. If you ever tried this it would only yield action without words.

Today, there is a changing climax in our culture, especially when it comes to religion. In the expression of one's religion and beliefs, what we see and enjoy is a freedom. However, it is without the consciousness that it has not always been so for the generations before us. If we look and compare those who readily attend worship services to those who will not, one excuse would be the availability of time. Admittedly, no matter how convenient services have become, some still won't attend.

Those who have shunned assemblies have forgotten the prayers of the elderly (the forgotten warriors). The prayers have allowed them yet another chance at life. These same prayers have been the cane, which has kept many from tripping or, better yet, falling off the curb of life. This culture has faced and emerged from dilemma after dilemma, all based on what they view as the circle of life. Their belief that time is doomed to repeat itself sustains their expectances.

Although we, the children of promise, know that the Lord delivers in a time of crisis, every eye is looking towards and every ear is peaked towards God. In fact, every ear should be turned and eyes should be focused on God's word always, not just during worldly calamities.

It is during a crisis that the exercise of prayer becomes most important because prayer is

1. **The natural atmosphere and the perspective for divine activity.**

In the midst of prayer, the miraculous occurs as in **John 11:41 - 43 (KJV)** *[41]Then they took away the stone from the place where the dead was laid. And Jesus lifted up his eyes, and said,*

Father, I thank thee that thou hast heard me. [42]And I knew that thou hearest me always: but because of the people which stand by I said it, that they may believe that thou hast sent me. [43]And when he thus had spoken, he cried with a loud voice, Lazarus, come forth.

2. **God's people know that in prayer their faith is action without limits.**

Things that we deem impossible are accomplished as in Gideon's case

Judges 6:37 - 40 (KJV) *[37]Behold, I will put a fleece of wool in the floor; and if the dew be on the fleece only, and it be dry upon all the earth beside, then shall I know that thou wilt save Israel by mine hand, as thou hast said. [38]And it was so: for he rose up early on the morrow, and thrust the fleece together, and wringed the dew out of the fleece, a bowl full of water. [39]And Gideon said unto God, Let not thine anger be hot against me, and I will speak but this once: let me prove, I pray thee, but this once with the fleece; let it now be dry only upon the fleece, and upon all the ground let there be dew. [40]And God did so that night: for it was dry upon the fleece only, and there was dew on all the ground.*

3. **It emphasizes your consummate power over your crisis.**

Frequently it seems hopeless, and you feel you should have given in. **Acts 16:25 - 26 (KJV)** *[25]And at midnight Paul and Silas prayed, and sang praises unto God: and the prisoners heard them. [26]And suddenly there was a great earthquake, so that the foundations of the prison were shaken: and immediately all the doors were opened, and every one's bands were loosed.*

David did it when he was without the family circle and established a relationship with God. The Shepherd boy David shows us "It's not what it looks like. Elisha did it when he was in a crisis and wanted his servant to know that when God gives you sight, He allows you to see that when He's more than any enemy against you can ever be. The Apostle Peter shares a lesson that, **"It's Not what it Looks Like"** because his testimony also reflects a repossession of sight.

Acts 12:6 - 11 (KJV) *[6]And when Herod would have brought him forth, the same night Peter was sleeping between two soldiers, bound with two chains: and the keepers before the door kept the prison. [7]And, behold, the angel of the Lord came upon him, and a light shined in the prison: and he smote Peter on the side, and raised him up, saying, Arise up quickly. And his chains fell off* *from his hands. ⁸And the angel said unto him, Gird thyself, and bind on thy sandals. And so he did. And he saith unto him, Cast thy garment about thee, and follow me. ⁹And he went out, and followed him; and wist not that it was true which was done by the angel; but thought he saw a vision. ¹⁰When they were past the first and the second ward, they came unto the iron gate that leadeth unto the city; which opened to them of his own accord: and they went out, and passed on through one street; and forthwith the angel departed from him. ¹¹And when Peter was come to himself, he said, Now I know of a surety, that the Lord hath sent his angel, and hath delivered me out of the hand of Herod, and from all the expectation of the people of the Jews.*

What Peter said was "Now I See! Herod was out to end the spreading of the Gospel. First he had James, the brother of John, beheaded, and then had the Apostle arrested and placed in prison. As ruler of the time Herod planned to execute him also. He places the Apostle under a secure guard of four squads of four soldiers each (16 altogether) and orders them to rotate in three-hour shifts to avoid sleep.

The scripture tells us that Peter was sleeping and that meant either he had given up hope or had remarkable composure. It suggests the story of the messenger named Jonah, who was asleep in the bottom of the boat while a storm raged *Jonah 1:5 (KJV) Then the mariners were afraid, and cried every man unto his god, and cast forth the wares that were in the ship into the sea, to lighten it of them. But Jonah was gone down into the sides of the ship; and he lay, and was fast asleep.* What Peter did was give us a lesson on peace of mind as a result of confidence in God.

What the next day held for Peter was not a secret. Herod's intentions were known, so Peter had no reason to expect a lesser fate. Yet he sleeps quietly without fear or worry. In fact, Peter was bound between two soldiers; his left hand chained to the right hand of one soldier and his right hand to the left of the other, the way Romans commonly secured prisoners. Two others, who had to watch the door of the prison, also guarded him, and he is sleeping. Symbolically **unemployment has one hand tied up, and the economic failure has the other. Business closures and home foreclosure are watching the door, and you can sleep.**

Scripture consistently uses a phrase to introduce angelic appearances or divine intervention: "Suddenly" or "Behold"

Acts 1:10 (KJV) *[10]And while they looked stedfastly toward heaven as he went up, behold, two men stood by them in white apparel;*

114

Acts 10:30 (KJV) *[30]And Cornelius said, Four days ago I was fasting until this hour; and at the ninth hour I prayed in my house, and, behold, a man stood before me in bright clothing,*

Luke 2:25 - 26 (KJV) *[25]And, behold, there was a man in Jerusalem, whose name was Simeon; and the same man was just and devout, waiting for the consolation of Israel: and the Holy Ghost was upon him. [26]And it was revealed unto him by the Holy Ghost, that he should not see death, before he had seen the Lord's Christ.*

Peter got his behold: **Acts 12:7 (KJV)** *[7]And, behold, the angel of the Lord came upon him, and a light shined in the prison:*

We know that "behold" cannot be too far away. The things that mean you no good and seek to end your life cannot keep us awake at night any longer. We can sleep in peace, knowing we are children of Promise. If the enemy does not understand, we know it's not what it looks like. God has given us vision to see our help. Now that we see the divine intervention God has purposed for our life, we cannot help but shout, "BEHOLD!"

If you pray, say this prayer

"Light is about to shine in the midst of my circumstance. NO matter what my situation or how hopeless things may seem, God will come through for me. He sends angels in answer to fervent and persistent prayer to break loose the chain and set me free."

Know that prayer is an opportunity to bring our will into line with God's plan Prayer is speaking to God. Prayer is an awesome privilege. Prayer is far better than complaining to each other. The dialogue, which is essential to our prayer, makes the difference. The voice sounded with conviction gathers God's attention when we speak His words. God is viewed as desiring to provoke blessing **James 1:5 (KJV)** *⁵If any of you lack wisdom, let him ask of God, that giveth to all men liberally, and upbraideth not; and it shall be given him.* The term "upbraideth" means whatever you have done prior, God forgives. Ever though He knows what you are going to do going forward, He still forgives and blesses you. Prayer will lead to a greater communion with God and a greater understanding of His will as it restores spiritual vision and heals physical blindness

Prayer shows humility and honesty:

2 Chronicles 6:14 (KJV) He prayed¹⁴And said, O LORD God of Israel, there is no God like thee in the heaven, nor in the earth; which keepest covenant, and showest mercy unto thy servants, that walk before thee with all their hearts:

Prayer recognizes the spiritual warfare around us and is not an escape from the world:

Matthew 5:13-16 (KJV) *[13]Ye are the salt of the earth: but if the salt have lost his savour, wherewith shall it be salted? it is thenceforth good for nothing, but to be cast out, and to be trodden under foot of men. [14]Ye are the light of the world. A city that is set on an hill cannot be hid. [15]Neither do men light a candle, and put it under a bushel, but on a candlestick; and it giveth light unto all that are in the house. [16]Let your light so shine before men, that they may see your good works, and glorify your Father which is in heaven.*

The angel smote Peter on the side, and raised him up, saying, "Arise up quickly," and his chains fell off from his hands.

Peter is then told, "Gird thyself" and "Bind thy sandals," Which mean that we need to start dressing for our pending victory. We must be prepared to follow without questioning or complaining. The putting on of the sandals is to prepare us to walk; we cannot get the victory if we are not willing or ready to move.

Peter was astonished because of the unexpected. Something wonderful had happened. It blew his mind so much that he thought it to be a vision. The soldiers stationed in the room and at intervals in the prison were passed silently because God sent a deep sleep over them to allow for Peter's escape. **The things that are holding you and me will be frozen and rendered helpless as God begin to loose us from their grip.** The Iron Gate that leads to the city will be open. The prison was situated between two walls, and the entrance to the prison inner wall opened directly into the city. Moreover, it opened spontaneously without any force or key because the hand of the Lord opens doors that no man can close. Peter passed through safe from any danger and without pursuit.

Acts 12:11 (KJV) [11] And when Peter was come to himself, he said, Now I know of a surety, that the Lord hath sent his angel, and hath delivered me out of the hand of Herod, and from all the expectation of the people of the Jews. Peter was now able to see as now we see. Because of prayer and the assembly of those who pray, divine intervention occurs. He prayed, and others prayed for the overcoming of those things which have imprisoned or held us captive.

Chapter 8

Thinking Like a Winner

~Man alone cannot measure my ability or
decide my fate, but my purpose can influence many people~

Many are striving to catch up with their spiritual side and celebrate the promise and fulfillment of the blessings which God has spoken. They can gain an understanding of what the prophet Jeremiah meant in disclosing this fact:

Jeremiah 29:11-14 (KJV) ¹¹*For I know the thoughts that I think toward you, saith the LORD, thoughts of peace, and not of evil, to give you an expected end.* ¹²*Then shall ye call upon me, and ye shall go and pray unto me, and I will hearken unto you.* ¹³*And ye shall seek me, and find me, when ye shall search for me with all your heart.* ¹⁴*And I will be found of you, saith the LORD: and*

I will turn away your captivity, and I will gather you from all the nations…

It is important to remember what we think about determines what we do. Even more importantly, the scripture tell us that what we think about shapes our attitudes and how we live our lives. Remember **God's Spirit** hovered over the waters: **Genesis 1:3 (KJV)** *³And God said, Let there be light: and there was light.* The Spirit of God is present everywhere. God gives us a brand new day every twenty-four (24) hours, and we seldom begin it with a brand new outlook. What happens at day's end as we kneel at our bedsides or lie in our beds and pray? *"Heavenly Father, please forgive me for my short comings and watch over me while I sleep. Lord, speak words of wisdom to guide me towards another day."* Then we rest and the troubles of that day are forgotten or are they?

In the morning, we may see a different date on the calendar, but the day ahead seems filled with the same routine, same troubles, same focus, same responsibilities, and same ideas. What we thought should have occurred did not, and we begin to doubt if God really did hear our prayers. But remember, you are still connected spiritually.

What do you do when you think God has not heard you, or his response is not as timely as you or your situation requires? You read in **Psalms 119:89** *Your word, O Lord is eternal; it stands firm in the heavens.* You hear in messages **Romans 12:2** *Be ye transformed by the renewing of your mind.* You speak it: "Yea in all things, we are more than conquerors," and we even declare it, "My name is victory."

Do you think that you have done all God has required of you? **Proverbs 3:6 (KJV)** *⁶In all thy ways acknowledge him, and he shall direct thy paths.* Yet you wonder if He has heard you! A key question during all of this is **"What are you thinking?"** Most of us can look around and find reminders of good intentions, and we see areas where we never followed what we were inspired or led to do in our spirit simply because we did not think the time was right.

The time God gives to us is ours to spend; we determine how to use it. In twenty-four hours there are 14,440 minutes and 86,400 seconds. Our days are hinged together in a unique way all according to God's word. We, in fact, have been guilty of holding our way of thinking captive all because of yesterday's pain and sorrow or its disappointments while wondering if God has thought about us.

In the 29ᵗʰ Chapter of Jeremiah, the prophet wrote a letter to a people who thought God had forgotten them and their prayers.

They were taken into captivity and lived in a society where they had worked, built homes, and birthed children. Their children married and produced children. On many days while they may have been going through, they did not observe the commandments of their heritage and have faith, if they had, God would have delivered them because He heard their prayers.

2 Chronicles 7:14 (KJV) *14If my people, which are called by my name, shall humble themselves, and pray, and seek my face....* I find myself asking a question about them and their mind set and wonder, **"What could they have been thinking?"** Some have turned on their signal lights but have missed their turn.

These people had homes that could be taken and worked in professions from which they could be fired or laid off. They helplessly struggled with stereo- types and forms of discrimination, were cheated, robbed, and abused. They were lied about and lied to. They formed groups for protection and went to con artists and scammers for direction and advice. They watched those in the world around them and believed that what others had was what they wanted.

What were they thinking? All this was and is a condition of captivity. Therefore, Jeremiah writes a letter to those with titles: elders, priests, and prophets. He addresses all the people who would hear, exclaiming **"God's News."** **Your** confinement, your time of disgrace and exile are at an end. It may have seemed hard, but your stripping away was necessary to reveal something to you. I had to uncover some things before you could discover promise. This is what the Lord Almighty; the God of Israel said then sent a message: "Your Seventy years are at an end."

When you compare some facts from the nineteenth century to the twenty-first century (i.e.1939, 1940 to 2009, 2010), you realize that although things were much cheaper then, the needs were still the same. People had to work, eat, own, and buy. The world had entered a period where there was prejudice, wars, and famine, but the Churches of that era whose leaders were the likes of T.T. Martin and A.W. Pink, stepped up and began to proclaim:

"We profit from the Word when we learn that the world is an enemy to be resisted and overcome." The Christian is bidden to "fight the good fight of faith" (1 Tim. 6:12), which implies that there are foes to be met and vanquished. (A.W. Pink)

T.T. Martin: began to use large tents for his meetings because most of the churches could not accommodate the crowds. Soon invita-

tions began to come from all sections of the country.

These were among the people who stepped into the pulpit and began preaching and conveying messages of hope, reassurance and promise, and the nation and the people of God responded. The way of thinking then changed, and people came out of depression and strife all because men and women of God stopped complaining and started proclaiming. They stopped separating and abandoning and started gathering and re-examining. Their words spoke truth to the people of God: "you're not forgotten, you're on God's mind! It all begins with your Spirit.

Jeremiah 29:11-14 (KJV) [11]For I know the thoughts that I think toward you, saith the LORD, thoughts of peace, and not of evil, to give you an expected end.

What have you been thinking? *[12]Then shall ye call upon me, and ye shall go and pray unto me, and I will hearken unto you.* What have you been thinking? *[13]And ye shall seek me, and find me, when ye shall search for me with all your heart.* What have you been thinking? *[14]And I will be found of you, saith the LORD: and I will turn away your captivity, and I will gather you from all the nations.*

What have you been thinking? I am coming out of captivity. It has been seventy years! As a condition of one coming out of captivity, not everyone endured seventy years, and what remained were and are called a **REMNANT PEOPLE** (small number with remaining quality). You are quality!

Our preceding generations endured their captivity until their coming out as the continually lifted us up in prayer. They prayed that we not be overtaken or absorbed by the culture of the world around us. They prayed that we as their descendents would remain on the path that lead to the fulfillment of God's promises because of what His thoughts are towards and about us.

We often do not know our own minds, but the Lord is never uncertain concerning His thoughts towards us. All that we have been thinking fails in comparison to God's thinking.

Psalms 40:5 (KJV) [5] *Many, O LORD my God, are thy wonderful works which thou hast done, and thy thoughts which are to us-ward: they cannot be reckoned up in order unto thee: if I would declare and speak of them, they are more than can be numbered.* God's thoughts cannot be numbered.

Psalms 139:17 (KJV) [17] *How precious also are thy thoughts unto me, O God! how great is the sum of them!* God's thoughts are precious.

Isaiah 55:9 (KJV) [9]*For as the heavens are higher than the earth, so are my ways higher than your ways, and my thoughts than your thoughts.* God's thoughts are above whatever we could ever imagine.

Jeremiah 23:5-6 (KJV) [5]*Behold, the days come, saith the LORD, that I will raise unto David a righteous Branch, and a King shall reign and prosper, and shall execute judgment and justice in the earth.* [6]*In his days Judah shall be saved, and Israel shall dwell safely: and this is his name whereby he shall be called,* **THE LORD OUR RIGHTEOUSNESS.**

The many thoughts we have had concerning right from wrong or good from bad have not turned God's intentions towards us. There's a story about a man who is on a luxury liner and suddenly he falls overboard, and no one sees him falling. He can't swim, and in desperation he begins calling for help. Now it just so happens there are several would-be rescuers on deck who hear his cries.

The first person is a **Sunday school teacher** who sees the man in the water she immediately reaches into her briefcase and pulls out a book on how to swim. She tosses it to the man and yells, "Now brother, you read that and follow the instructions, and you'll be alright."

The second person is a **mother** who sees the man in the water. She immediately jumps into the water and begins to swim around the drowning man saying, "Now just watch me swim, do as I do, and you'll be alright."

The next person happens to be a member of the **trustee board** who looks at the man's situation with deep concern and yells out, "Now brother just hold on; help is on the way. We're going to establish a committee and discuss your problem, and if we come up with the proper financing, we'll resolve your dilemma."

The next person happens to be a **deacon** who, thinking positively yells to the drowning man; "Friend, this situation is not nearly as bad as you think. Just think dry.

A nearby **Usher** sees that the man by this time is going down for the third time and is desperately waving his arms yells. He out, "Yes brother, I see that hand. Is there another? Is there another?"

And finally, the last person on deck **"could be you"**, who immediately plunges into the water at the risk of your own life and pulls the man to safety.

"If God can use anybody, He can use me" should be more than a phrase. As the body of

Christ, we must all know the steps and be completely focused on and attentive to the Word of the Lord, not only just to learn it, but also to live it!

In this alone have the assurance that we will be victorious, and we will make it to our destiny. What have you been thinking? Did you not know that the seeds which are generations to follow **will be blessed and are blessed** through and by our prayers.

Jeremiah 30:18-22 (KJV) *¹⁸Thus saith the LORD; Behold, I will bring again the captivity of Jacob's tents, and have mercy on his dwelling places; and the city shall be builded upon her own heap, and the palace shall remain after the manner thereof. ¹⁹And out of them shall proceed thanksgiving and the voice of them that make merry: and I will multiply them, and they shall not be few; I will also glorify them, and they shall not be small. ²⁰Their children also shall be as aforetime, and their congregation shall be established before me, and I will punish all that oppress them. ²¹And their nobles shall be of themselves, and their governor shall proceed from the midst of them; and I will cause him to draw near, and he shall approach unto me: for who is this that engaged his heart to approach unto me? saith the LORD. ²²And ye shall be my people, and I will be your God.*

Its time that we understand that our way of thinking and what we have been thinking have been released from captivity. Your seventy years are at an end, and we're coming out. We cannot allow the empty promises of the world's definition of success to hold us back. When we realize that God Almighty has thought of our situation, it has an expected end. When we grasp onto the promise, it shall come to pass. Do not be depressed and over- come, give God praise and become an over-comer: *"¹¹For I know the thoughts that I think toward you, saith the LORD, thoughts of peace, and not of evil, to give you an expected end.* To get to the end, there has to be a beginning. It starts today by changing your way of thinking, you must think like a winner!

Chapter 9

Your Next Step

*~We stumble aimlessly around often shielding our
Eyes from light and craving light in
Darkness. Faith waits to be our
Shade in the sun and our light
In the dark. All we must do is
Turn it on."~*

There was an annual event once held in New York where runners gathered at the base of the Empire State Building, and formed a congregation. They meet at the base of its stairs, which total 1,576, to be exact, and they waited on the beginning of a race to reach the top. Many contestants and visitors have stated that the view from such elevation is breath-taking, but it is not the view they come for.

These participants have one objective, to reach the top as fast as they can. Their techniques may vary in accomplishing this feat. Some may include skipping two or three steps at a time all because the objective is to reach the top and stand in victory!

1 Corinthians 9:24(KJV) ²⁴ Do you not know that those who run in a race all run, but one receives the prize? Run in such a way that you may obtain it.

I wonder if this thought is on their minds, but I doubt it. During this event, some participants are often injured in their pursuit of victory. It is my hope that in the pursuit of your spirit that you too will stand atop the mountaintop and shout triumphantly.

During one race, a woman broke her arm and still finished the race before seeking medical aid. A 93-year-old man said, "I've never made it to the top, but I'll come back every year as long as God gives me the strength until I make it!" That is dedication to a cause. Can your pursuit be spoken of with the same conviction?

David in Psalm 131 also speaks of a gathering of a congregation at the base of a staircase, which consisted of only fifteen steps. They were not there to race, but they, too, had a purpose for reaching the top.

¹ LORD, my heart is not haughty, Nor my eyes lofty. Neither do I concern myself with great matters, Nor with things too profound for me. ²

Surely I have calmed and quieted my soul, Like a weaned child with his mother; Like a weaned child is my soul within me.³ O Israel, hope in the Lord *From this time forth and forever.*

This scripture speaks of these fifteen steps, which are similar to the number of Psalms, called "the Songs of Degrees." Those who had not seen the joy at the annual ceremony of the water drawing had not seen rejoicing in their lives. Those individuals, in effect, mirror many today. Season after season there is no joy, but the continual slow trod forward much like an ox pulling the millstone to ground wheat. Who would not enjoy the ascent to a point where when God hears your prayers, He leans over from Heaven to respond because in you He hears His own voice?

Upon these steps stood the Levite musicians who played their musical instruments, playing harmoniously the fifteen "Songs of Ascent" Psalms 120-134 these are the same fifteen "Songs of Ascent" sung by the Levites while ascending the fifteen stairs in the Temple. Thus the elevation of fifteen represented the transition from <u>physical</u> to <u>spiritual</u>. In the physical act of moving and ascending, you grow closer to the Holy of Holies, closer to the Presence of God, closer to your Spirit.

Affirmed biblically as a royal priesthood in our daily walk we many times stand at the base of the steps. What is your next step? Each psalm presents an occasion for entering the presence of God fifteen steps.

Step One: Affliction in Psalms *120 (KJV)*
How often has difficulty occurred and caused you not to even attempt to stand on this step?

¹ In my distress I cried unto the LORD, and he heard me. ² Deliver my soul, O LORD, from lying lips, and from a deceitful tongue. ³ What shall be given unto thee? Or what shall be done unto thee, thou false tongue? ⁴ Sharp arrows of the mighty, with coals of juniper. ⁵ Woe is me, that I sojourn in Mesech, that I dwell in the tents of Kedar! ⁶ My soul hath long dwelt with him that hateth peace. ⁷ I am for peace: but when I speak, they are for war.

Step Two: Looking to God *Psalms 121 (KJV)*
These words have more effect when you do stand and look from a higher perspective. On your knees may be fine in certain situations, but it will take the turning over to see God and even pulling yourself to your feet. Approaching this second step is key.

¹ I will lift up mine eyes unto the hills, from whence cometh my help. ² My help cometh from the LORD, which made heaven and earth. ³ He will not suffer thy foot to be moved: he that keepeth thee will not slumber. ⁴ Behold, he that keepeth Israel shall neither slumber nor sleep. ⁵ The LORD is thy keeper: the LORD is thy shade upon thy right hand. ⁶ The sun shall not smite thee by day, nor the moon by night. ⁷ The LORD shall preserve thee from all evil: he shall preserve thy soul. ⁸ The LORD shall preserve thy going out and thy coming in from this time forth, and even for evermore.

Step Three: Joy in communion
Psalms 122 (KJV)

How often have you said that not everyone can be a source of comfort in times of adversity? How is it then that when the very vessels containing the healing ointment are within the steps of the church that many stand without?

¹ I was glad when they said unto me, Let us go into the house of the LORD. ² Our feet shall stand within thy gates, O Jerusalem. ³ Jerusalem is builded as a city that is compact together: ⁴ Whither the tribes go up, the tribes of the LORD, unto the testimony of Israel, to give thanks unto the name of the LORD. ⁵ For there are set thrones of judgment, the thrones of the house of

David. ⁶ *Pray for the peace of Jerusalem: they shall prosper that love thee. ⁷ Peace be within thy walls, and prosperity within thy palaces. ⁸ For my brethren and companions' sakes, I will now say, Peace be within thee. ⁹ Because of the house of the LORD our God I will seek thy good.*

Step Four: Invocation *Psalms 123 (KJV)*

The very inviting of God to solve your problems lies within knowing that God has allowed no problem that can hinder you to be formed unless He already has an answer for it. Have you invited Him in?

¹ *Unto thee lift I up mine eyes, O thou that dwellest in the heavens. ² Behold, as the eyes of servants look unto the hand of their masters, and as the eyes of a maiden unto the hand of her mistress; so our eyes wait upon the LORD our God, until that he have mercy upon us. ³ Have mercy upon us, O LORD, have mercy upon us: for we are exceedingly filled with contempt. ⁴ Our soul is exceedingly filled with the scorning of those that are at ease, and with the contempt of the proud.*

Step Five: Thanksgiving *Psalms 124 (KJV)*

The very reason to thank someone is for the assistance which was rendered to aid you. It

begins by knowing there is nothing you could
have done on your own.

*[1] If it had not been the LORD who was on our
side, now may Israel say; [2] If it had not been
the LORD who was on our side, when men rose
up against us: [3] Then they had swallowed us
up quick, when their wrath was kindled against
us: [4] Then the waters had overwhelmed us, the
stream had gone over our soul: [5] Then the proud
waters had gone over our soul. [6] Blessed be the
LORD, who hath not given us as a prey to their
teeth. [7] Our soul is escaped as a bird out of the
snare of the fowlers: the snare is broken, and we
are escaped. [8] Our help is in the name of the
LORD, who made heaven and earth.*

Step Six: Confidence, *Psalms 125 (KJV)*
There are many burdens that would weaken a
person not prepared to carry, but God's ability
rests within us all. The look in the reflecting
laver should have many washing their faces of
tears and standing with confidence before those
who counted them out God made a way
for you to stand within.

*[1] They that trust in the LORD shall be as mount
Zion, which cannot be removed, but abideth
for ever. [2] As the mountains are round about
Jerusalem, so the LORD is round about his*

people from henceforth even for ever. ³ *For the rod of the wicked shall not rest upon the lot of the righteous; lest the righteous put forth their hands unto iniquity.* ⁴ *Do good, O LORD, unto those that be good, and to them that are upright in their hearts.* ⁵ *As for such as turn aside unto their crooked ways, the LORD shall lead them forth with the workers of iniquity: but peace shall be upon Israel.*

Step Seven: Patiently waiting for deliverance
Psalms 126 (KJV)
Where would we be if not for the very strength that lies in staying power? During adversity, know deliverance will come.

¹ *When the LORD turned again the captivity of Zion, we were like them that dream.* ² *Then was our mouth filled with laughter, and our tongue with singing: then said they among the heathen, The LORD hath done great things for them.* ³ *The LORD hath done great things for us; whereof we are glad.* ⁴ *Turn again our captivity, O LORD, as the streams in the south.* ⁵ *They that sow in tears shall reap in joy.* ⁶ *He that goeth forth and weepeth, bearing precious seed, shall doubtless come again with rejoicing, bringing his sheaves with him.*

Step Eight: God's grace and favor
Psalms 127 (KJV)
What we receive on a daily basis is a sure dose
of strength, not because of who we are but
because of whose we are.

[1] *Except the LORD build the house, they labour
in vain that build it: except the LORD keep the
city, the watchman waketh but in vain.* [2] *It is
vain for you to rise up early, to sit up late, to
eat the bread of sorrows: for so he giveth his
beloved sleep.* [3] *Lo, children are an heritage
of the LORD: and the fruit of the womb is his
reward.* [4] *As arrows are in the hand of a mighty
man; so are children of the youth.* [5] *Happy is
the man that hath his quiver full of them: they
shall not be ashamed, but they shall speak with
the enemies in the gate.*

Step Nine: Fear of the Lord **Psalms 128 (KJV)**
Many steps are taken without regard to what
will happen, but treading upon a place of
goodness enables every blessing to fall upon us.

[1] *Blessed is every one that feareth the LORD;
that walketh in his ways.* [2] *For thou shalt eat
the labour of thine hands: happy shalt thou be,
and it shall be well with thee.* [3] *Thy wife shall be
as a fruitful vine by the sides of thine house: thy
children like olive plants round about thy table.*

⁴ *Behold, that thus shall the man be blessed that feareth the LORD.* ⁵ *The LORD shall bless thee out of Zion: and thou shalt see the good of Jerusalem all the days of thy life.* ⁶ *Yea, thou shalt see thy children's children, and peace upon Israel.*

Step Ten: Martyrdom *Psalms 129 (KJV)*
What we often go through won't reflect the growth that we underwent to make it through because the hands of God hold us tight during times of threat.

¹ *Many a time have they afflicted me from my youth, may Israel now say:* ² *Many a time have they afflicted me from my youth: yet they have not prevailed against me.* ³ *The plowers plowed upon my back: they made long their furrows.* ⁴ *The LORD is righteous: he hath cut asunder the cords of the wicked.* ⁵ *Let them all be confounded and turned back that hate Zion.* ⁶ *Let them be as the grass upon the housetops, which withereth afore it groweth up:* ⁷ *Wherewith the mower filleth not his hand; nor he that bindeth sheaves his bosom.* ⁸ *Neither do they which go by say, The blessing of the LORD be upon you: we bless you in the name of the LORD.*

Step Eleven: Hatred of sins **Psalms 130 (KJV)**
The hopes that we enjoy are to always agree
with God's word which reminds us that we are
what we are. We must confess to what
we have done.

*¹ Out of the depths have I cried unto thee, O
LORD. ² Lord, hear my voice: let thine ears be
attentive to the voice of my supplications. ³ If
thou, LORD, shouldest mark iniquities, O Lord,
who shall stand? ⁴ But there is forgiveness with
thee, that thou mayest be feared. ⁵ I wait for the
LORD, my soul doth wait, and in his word do I
hope. ⁶ My soul waiteth for the Lord more than
they that watch for the morning: I say, more than
they that watch for the morning. ⁷ Let Israel hope
in the LORD: for with the LORD there is mercy,
and with him is plenteous redemption. ⁸ And he
shall redeem Israel from all his iniquities.*

Step Twelve: Humility **Psalms 131 KJV)**
This is the step within our sight. Our best
action to climb it is to consider others first. It is
the step where you might have to tarry a little
longer, and the step will not seem as wide as the
others might. It may even appear a little narrow
compared to the others and harder to maintain
your footing. While people are judging, and you
are not reacting, God is rewarding, so stay on
this step a little longer. The humility we show

makes us unlike the world although we are in it. As a result, what God has for us will be received with the spirit of excellence.

¹ LORD, my heart is not haughty, nor mine eyes lofty: neither do I exercise myself in great matters, or in things too high for me. ² Surely I have behaved and quieted myself, as a child that is weaned of his mother: my soul is even as a weaned child. ³ Let Israel hope in the LORD from henceforth and for ever.

Step thirteen: Desire for the coming of Christ
Psalms 132 (KJV)
This is reaching the pinnacle of seeing the glorious works that God has prepared for us and the habitation of our rest.

¹ LORD, remember David, and all his afflictions: ² How he sware unto the LORD, and vowed unto the mighty God of Jacob; ³ Surely I will not come into the tabernacle of my house, nor go up into my bed; ⁴ I will not give sleep to mine eyes, or slumber to mine eyelids, ⁵ Until I find out a place for the LORD, an habitation for the mighty God of Jacob. ⁶ Lo, we heard of it at Ephratah: we found it in the fields of the wood. ⁷ We will go into his tabernacles: we will worship at his footstool. ⁸ Arise, O LORD, into thy rest; thou, and the ark of thy strength. ⁹ Let thy priests be clothed with righteousness; and let thy saints shout for joy. [10] For thy servant David's sake turn not away the face of thine anointed. [11] The LORD hath sworn in truth unto David; he will not turn from it; Of the fruit of thy body will I set upon thy throne. [12] If thy children will keep my covenant and my testimony that I shall teach them, their children shall also sit upon thy throne for evermore. [13] For the LORD hath chosen Zion; he hath desired it for his habitation. [14] This is my rest for ever: here will I dwell; for I have desired it. [15] I will abundantly bless her provision: I will satisfy her poor with bread. [16] I will also clothe her priests with salvation: and her saints shall shout aloud for joy. [17] There will I make the horn of David to bud: I have ordained a lamp for mine anointed. [18] His enemies will I clothe with shame: but upon himself shall his crown flourish.

Step Fourteen: Concord and charity
Psalms 133 (KJV)
I can never alone to ponder what I could
have been if I did not consider those
I could have helped.

[1] Behold, how good and how pleasant it is for brethren to dwell together in unity! [2] It is like the precious ointment upon the head, that ran down upon the beard, even Aaron's beard: that went

down to the skirts of his garments; [3] *As the dew of Hermon, and as the dew that descended upon the mountains of Zion: for there the LORD commanded the blessing, even life for evermore.*

Step Fifteen: Constant blessing of God
Psalms 134(KJV)
I have not been selfish, envious, greedy, or lacking because not all God has allowed me to receive was ever meant for me alone.

[1] *Behold, bless ye the LORD, all ye servants of the LORD, which by night stand in the house of the LORD.* [2] *Lift up your hands in the sanctuary, and bless the LORD.* [3] *The LORD that made heaven and earth bless thee out of Zion.*

The number fifteen is found in scripture and the apostolic writings, parables, and other forms, which are symbolic. We hear and receive and already understand the significance of the numbers seven, eight and others, but how many are aware of the significance of the **number fifteen**?

It is not a number often encountered in scripture, and its obscurity has not made it a candidate for deep study. However, even this number has spiritual significance and meaning associated with it. The number "**fifteen**" is most often used to **symbolize deliverance**, along with promises of restoration, restitution, healing, and the constant blessings of God.

When we consider Psalm 131 by David, who is the author and the subject of it, many incidents of his life may be employed to illustrate it. This is one of the shortest Psalms to read, but one of the longest to learn, because it speaks of a young child. However, it contains the experiences of a man in Christ. It speaks of lowliness and humility, which are viewed in connection with a sanctified heart, a will subdued to the mind of God and a hope looking to the Lord alone.

Happy are the man and woman who can without falsehood use these words as their own. They wear about themselves the likeness of our Lord, who said, "I am meek and lowly in heart." The Psalm is in advance of all the "Songs of Degrees," which have preceded it, for lowliness is one of the highest attainments in the divine life. These steps reflected in the "Song of Degrees are but a short ladder if we count the words. Yet they rise to a great height, reaching from deep humility.

As we climb these steps, what step are you on? As you think about your walk to the twelve steps where the title humility is established, consider how important is it to you?

Humility is the proper attitude before God. When our lives fall apart, we also should turn to God for direction and help. Like Joshua and the elders, we should humble ourselves so that we will be able to hear his words.

Joshua 7:6 (KJV) *⁶And Joshua rent his clothes, and fell to the earth upon his face before the ark of the LORD until the eventide, he and the elders of Israel, and put dust upon their heads.* (We all have our own city of Ai)

Humility keeps us from depending on our own strengths. Too often, we rely on our own skills and strength, especially when the task before us seems easy. We go to God only when the obstacles seem too great. However, only God knows what lies ahead. Consulting him, even when we are on a winning streak, may save us from grave mistakes or misjudgments. God may want us to learn lessons, remove pride, or consult others before he will work through us.

Humility makes our prayers direct and honest. Hiding your needs from God is ignoring the only one who can really help. God welcomes your honest prayers and wants you to express your true feelings to him. Any believer can become more honest in prayer by remembering that God is all knowing and all-powerful and that his love is everlasting. *2 Chronicles 7:14 (KJV)* *¹⁴If my people, which are called by my name, shall humble themselves, and pray, and seek my face, and turn from their wicked ways; then will I* *hear from heaven, and will forgive their sin, and will heal their land.*

Humility is good training in obedience and challenges our pride. Naaman, a great hero, was used to getting respect; therefore, he was outraged when Elisha treated him like an ordinary person. A proud man, he expected royal treatment. To wash in a great river would be one thing, but the Jordan was small and dirty. To wash in the Jordan, Naaman thought, was beneath a man of his position. Naaman had to humble himself and obey Elisha's commands in order to be healed. *2 Kings 5:14 - 15 (KJV)* *[14]Then went he down, and dipped himself seven times in Jordan, according to the saying of the man of God: and his flesh came again like unto the flesh of a little child, and he was clean. [15]And he returned to the man of God, he and all his company, and came, and stood before him: and he said, Behold, now I know that there is no God in all the earth, but in Israel: now therefore, I pray thee, take a blessing of thy servant.*

Humility clarifies our dependence on God. Obedience to God begins with humility. We must believe that his way is better than our own. We may not always understand his ways of working, but by humbly obeying, we will receive his blessings. We must remember that

(1) God's ways are best
(2) God wants our obedience more than anything else does; and
(3) God can use anything to accomplish his purposes.

Humility is a deep awareness of unworthiness, not worthlessness. When we look at the vast expanse of creation, we wonder how God could be concerned for people who constantly disappoint him. Yet God created us only a little lower than himself or the angels! The next time you question your worth as a person, remember that God considers you highly valuable. We have great worth because we bear the stamp of the Creator. Because God has already declared how valuable we are to him, we can be set free from feelings of worthlessness. *Luke 18:14 (KJV) [14]I tell you, this man went down to his house justified rather than the other: for every one that exalteth himself shall be abased; and he that humbleth himself shall be exalted.*
Humility increases our appreciation of God. To respect God's majesty, we must compare ourselves to his greatness. When we look at creation, we often feel small by comparison. To feel small is a healthy way to get back to reality, but God does not want us to dwell on our smallness. Humility means proper respect for God, not self-depreciation. *James 4:10 (KJV) [10]Humble*

yourselves in the sight of the Lord, and he shall lift you up.

Humility is essential for service to others. Jesus advised people not to rush for the best places at a feast. People today are just as eager to raise their social status, whether by being with the right people, dressing for success, or driving the right car. Whom do you try to impress? Rather than aiming for prestige, look for a place where you can serve. If God wants you to serve on a wider scale, he will invite you to take a higher place. *Psalms 51:17 (KJV)* [17] *The sacrifices of God are a broken spirit: a broken and a contrite heart, O God, thou wilt not despise.*

Jesus Christ is our model for humility. How can we humble ourselves? Some people try to give the appearance of humility in order to manipulate others. Others think that humility means putting themselves down. Truly humble people compare themselves only with Christ, realize their sinfulness, and understand their limitations.

On the other hand, they also recognize their gifts and strengths and are willing to use them as Christ directs. Humility is not self-degradation; it is realistic assessment and commitment to serve. *1 Corinthians 4:21 (KJV)* [21] *What will ye? shall I come unto you with a rod, or in love, and in the spirit of meekness?*

What step are you on? The steps behind humility are important, but humility leads to the desire for the coming of Christ, (Psalms.132) you cannot make it on your own. Your knowledge of concord and charity, (Psalms.133) I can get along with others and be a giver of both time and monies you are receiving the constant blessing of God. (Psalms.134) Who cannot stand constant blessings of health, wealth, wisdom, joy and peace? When you reach the fifteenth step of spiritual significance, you stand ready to receive. *1 Peter 5:6 (KJV) ⁶Humble yourselves therefore under the mighty hand of God, that he may exalt you in due time:*

Chapter 10

God's Ultimate Plan

*~ No matter how wonderfully I articulate my
Thoughts and plans, without seeking
God's purpose for my life, they will come
to nothing~*

The way of many has often been abandoned by lack of planning. Confusion sets in, which leads to panic and fear. On the battlefield of life, not many encounters are won without the skills of a great planner. Saul (Paul) was a troubled vessel in whom God's ultimate plan was revealed. In his period, there was a belief that the Messiah would be a powerful leader striking with the vengeance of God and a forceful arm. Even our generation has taken the concept as a "by any means necessary" message: *Matthew 11:12 (KJV) ¹²And from the days of John the Baptist until now the kingdom of heaven suffereth violence, and the violent take it by force.*

However, the literal words of the Bible often warn that those who live lives of violence will meet violent ends: **Psalms 7:16 (KJV)** *[16] His mischief shall return upon his own head, and his violent dealing shall come down upon his own fate.* God demanded an end to violence. ***Jeremiah 22:3 (KJV)*** *[3]Thus saith the LORD; Execute ye judgment and righteousness, and deliver the spoiled out of the hand of the oppressor: and do no wrong, do no violence to the stranger, the fatherless, nor the widow, neither shed innocent blood in this place.* Such violence was especially evidenced in the oppression of the poor by the rich in biblical transcripts: Micah **6:12 (KJV)** *[12]For the rich men thereof are full of violence and the inhabitants thereof have spoken lies, and their tongue is deceitful in their mouth.*

In and by God's ultimate plan, Saul, in his transition to Paul became a Christian. His prior education was enormously helpful because he was able to assimilate Christian doctrines rapidly and relate them accurately to the scriptural teaching he had received. He is described in *1 Timothy 3:3 (KJV): [3]Not given to wine, no striker, not greedy of filthy lucre; but patient, not a brawler, not covetous.* Paul's writing gives us a divine viewpoint of what Jesus did for you and me that made a difference. His account of how Jesus was delivered up in our stead provides focus of who we are, all according to the fixed Purpose and foreknowledge of God.

Because God alone has foreknowledge, nothing is hidden from Him. There is nothing from our past, present, or future that can evade His knowledge of us, and only the foolish think otherwise.

Jesus was crucified in our place and took upon Himself the total and complete penalty for all our sins and our own plans: past, present and future. When the price was completely paid, God then raised Him up, loosing Him from the pains, the agony, and travailing of death that He had suffered on our account. It was not possible for hell to contain Him once our price was paid.

David prophesied in **Psalm 16:8-11 (KJV):** *"I saw the Lord constantly before My face. He is at My right hand so that I cannot be overcome, Therefore, My heart is glad, and My tongue shouts for joy; moreover, My flesh also shall dwell in hope, for You will not abandon My soul, leaving it in hell, nor will You allow Your Holy One to decay. You have made known to me the ways of life; You fill Me with joy in Your presence and with eternal pleasures at Your right hand forever more"*

This tells me God has made known the path of life and fills me with joy in His presence. Nothing either significant or relevant to our being could ever occur without God's ultimate plan!

When the spirit part of us seems separated, it is to cause a reaction. Paul knew that the existence of God could easily be perceived by anyone, and his many trials did not deter him from living the Christian life. So Paul writes to the Ephesians and us today, "He didn't have to do it but He Did!"

***Ephesians 1:9-13* (KJV)** *[9]Having made known unto us the mystery of his will, according to his good pleasure which he hath purposed in himself: [10]That in the dispensation of the fulness of times he might gather together in one all things in Christ, both which are in heaven, and which are on earth; even in him: [11]In whom also we have obtained an inheritance, being predestinated according to the purpose of him who worketh all things after the counsel of his own will: [12]That we should be to the praise of his glory, who first trusted in Christ. [13]In whom ye also trusted, after that ye heard the word of truth, the gospel of your salvation: in whom also after that ye believed, ye were sealed with that Holy Spirit of promise.*

When I think about a plan, it is synonymous plot, formula, or system, project, or design. It implies a formulated method of doing something. A plan refers to any method of thinking out acts and purposes beforehand. What are your plans for today? A project is a proposed or tentative plan, often elaborate or all embracing.

Design suggests art, dexterity, or craft (sometimes evil and selfish) in the elaboration or execution of a plan, and often tends to emphasize the purpose in view. Paul explains the ultimate plan by God's design for our lives

The apostle Paul was imprisoned and writes to the church expressing that God has given us a glimpse of who we are, where we come from, and where we are going. But more importantly, Paul provides a vision to the church to focus on God's ultimate plan.

As a body, we, not buildings and locations, but we, the believers, are in position through grace that was predestined. Paul was in jail and under house arrest, and his movements were guarded. He had been imprisoned before with Silas. *Acts 16:22 - 23 (KJV)* ²²*And the multitude rose up together against them: and the magistrates rent off their clothes, and commanded to beat them.* ²³*And when they had laid many stripes upon them, they cast them into prison, charging the jailor to keep them safely:*

Paul writes concerning the Body of Christ. Our walk, in accordance with that position as Believers, allows us to hear the word of truth. We are saved through the preaching of the Gospel, and upon receiving salvation, we have been sealed. By witness of the Holy Spirit, we will obtain the promises of God.

1 Corinthians 2:9-10 (KJV) [9]But as it is written, Eye hath not seen, nor ear heard, neither have entered into the heart of man, the things which God hath prepared for them that love him. [10]But God hath revealed them unto us by his Spirit: for the Spirit searcheth all things, yea, the deep things of God.

Ephesians, in its entirety, is the fulfillment of this scripture as it reveals the things God has prepared for those who love Him. Paul explains what God has made known: *[9]Having made known unto us the mystery of his will, according to his good pleasure which he hath purposed in himself: God will becomes known because it pleases Him to show us what part He plays in our life's*

God's plan is eternal, meaning perpetual, true at all times, and characterized by abiding fellowship with Him. **Gen 9:12 (KJV)** *[12]And God said, This is the token of the covenant which I make between me and you and every living creature that is with you, for perpetual generations: God created me to live and walk in dominion.*

God has abundantly blessed me with good things of every kind and by His word has made me steward of His riches in this earth. God said,

"This is my word," and His word is so important that He places His word higher than His name:

Psa 138:2 (KJV) *2 I will worship toward thy holy temple, and praise thy name for thy loving-kindness and for thy truth: for thou hast magnified thy word above all thy name.*

Paul says;*10That in the dispensation of the fulness of times he might gather together in one all things in Christ, both which are in heaven, and which are on earth; even in him:*

In Christ, the treasures of this world and Heaven will come to pass because God is outside of time. In Christ, you become treasure to God, a spiritual treasure.

SPIRITUAL TREASURES

Proverbs 8:18 (KJV) 18Riches and honour are with me; yea, durable riches and righteousness. I walk the walk of righteousness and remain fixed on the paths of justice. I have been anointed to become affluent and wealthy; it is God's perfect will that all of my treasuries be full to the brim. Spiritual treasures are enduring.

God is the source of spiritual treasures: *Proverbs 10:22 (KJV) 22The blessing of the*

LORD, it maketh rich, and he addeth no sorrow with it.

My Father has blessed me with an abundance of wealth and eternal riches free of all of the troubles that the world must endure. I understand that I find great joy in the attainment of wisdom. In all things, I seek my Father's counsel, and He gives me all that I desire.

A paradox is a statement or proposition that seems self-contradictory or absurd but in reality expresses a possible truth. This was your life before Christ, a paradox, but now the time gives it proof.

Proverbs 13:7 (KJV) *⁷There is that maketh himself rich, yet hath nothing: there is that maketh himself poor, yet hath great riches.*

By the words of my mouth, I obtain and enjoy all good things. I am careful not to speak those things that would strip me of my blessings. I'll use my words to produce health, joy, love, peace, prosperity, and power in my life. My words shall be good ones.

I am guided by Spiritual vision: **Ephesians 1:18 (KJV)** *¹⁸The eyes of your understanding being enlightened; that ye may know what is the hope of his calling, and what the riches of the glory of his inheritance in the saints,*

Your spirit has been enlightened with a flood of understanding so you can now see and comprehend the hope of your calling "All things are placed under your feet, and every power and dominion must obey as you apply the power of attorney that Jesus has given you to use in his name.

God's elect received an inheritance: ***James 2:5 (KJV)*** *⁵Hearken, my beloved brethren, Hath not God chosen the poor of this world rich in faith, and heirs of the kingdom which he hath promised to them that love him?*

With all your heart profess your love of God. Because He loves you, do your best to see all things through His eyes. He has chosen you to be well supplied through faith and to inherit the Kingdom that He has promised you:

In whom also we have obtained an inheritance, being predestinated according to the purpose of him who worketh all things after the counsel of his own will:

The kingdom in which the Father resides and Christ is seated on His right hand is ours also through inheritance of eternal life. Paul contrasts our earthly bodies (earthly tents) and our future resurrection bodies (an eternal body) made for us by God himself and not by human hands

***We should be to the praise of his glory, who
first trusted in Christ.*** God the father thought
enough of us to trust His son to come down and
not change His mind once the process of paying
for our sins began.

Psalms 146:1-2 *Praise the Lord! Praise the
Lord; I tell myself, I will praise the Lord as long
as I live. I will sing praise to my God even with
my dying breath.*

When you praise, your heart is on God and
giving thanks to Him for who He is and what
Christ did and is doing. *Praise* comes from a Latin
word meaning "value" or "price." Therefore, to
give praise to God is to proclaim His merit or
worth:

1.   Praise takes our minds off our problems and
     shortcomings and focuses them on God:

1 Peter 1:3 - 9 (KJV) *³Blessed be the God and
Father of our Lord Jesus Christ, which according
to his abundant mercy hath begotten us again
unto a lively hope by the resurrection of Jesus
Christ from the dead, ⁴To an inheritance incor-
ruptible, and undefiled, and that fadeth not away,
reserved in heaven for you, ⁵Who are kept by
the power of God through faith unto salvation
ready to be revealed in the last time. ⁶Wherein*

ye greatly rejoice, though now for a season, if need be, ye are in heaviness through manifold temptations: [7]That the trial of your faith, being much more precious than of gold that perisheth, though it be tried with fire, might be found unto praise and honour and glory at the appearing of Jesus Christ: [8]Whom having not seen, ye love; in whom, though now ye see him not, yet believing, ye rejoice with joy unspeakable and full of glory: [9]Receiving the end of your faith, even the salvation of your souls.

2. Praise leads us from individual meditation to corporate worship:

Colossians 3:15 - 16 (KJV) *[15]And let the peace of God rule in your hearts, to the which also ye are called in one body; and be ye thankful. [16]Let the word of Christ dwell in you richly in all wisdom; teaching and admonishing one another in psalms and hymns and spiritual songs, singing with grace in your hearts to the Lord.*

3. Praise causes us to consider and appreciate God's character:

Psalms 113:1 - 5 (KJV) *[1] Praise ye the LORD. Praise, O ye servants of the LORD, praise the name of the LORD. [2] Blessed be the name of the LORD from this time forth and for evermore.*

³ From the rising of the sun unto the going down of the same the LORD'S name is to be praised. ⁴ The LORD is high above all nations, and his glory above the heavens. ⁵ Who is like unto the LORD our God, who dwelleth on high,

4. Praise lifts our perspective from the earthly to the heavenly:

Matthew 6:10 (KJV) *¹⁰Thy kingdom come. Thy will be done in earth, as it is in heaven.*

Our access to God has been secured because the Holy Spirit which resides within us connects us directly to God. The way to activate your access is hear the word. God holds all things together by His Word:

Ephesians 1:13 (KJV)*¹³In whom ye also trusted, after that ye heard the word of truth, the gospel of your salvation: in whom also after that ye believed, ye were sealed with that holy Spirit of promise.,*

Believe the word; the Word is a sure guide to us in any and every situation:

Psalms 119:105 (KJV) *¹⁰⁵ Thy word is a lamp unto my feet, and a light unto my path.*

Receive the word; God's Word shows us who we are and what we have in Christ.

James 1:23 - 25 (KJV) *[23]For if any be a hearer of the word, and not a doer, he is like unto a man beholding his natural face in a glass: [24]For he beholdeth himself, and goeth his way, and straightway forgetteth what manner of man he was. [25]But whoso looketh into the perfect law of liberty, and continueth therein, he being not a forgetful hearer, but a doer of the work, this man shall be blessed in his deed.*

We become one with God through the Word:

John 17:17 - 21 (KJV) *[17]Sanctify them through thy truth: thy word is truth. [18]As thou hast sent me into the world, even so have I also sent them into the world. [19]And for their sakes I sanctify myself, that they also might be sanctified through the truth. [20]Neither pray I for these alone, but for them also which shall believe on me through their word; [21]That they all may be one; as thou, Father, art in me, and I in thee, that they also may be one in us: that the world may believe that thou hast sent me.*

We may face adversity, persecution, afflic-tion, hardship or disaster, but God's remarkable purpose and ultimate plan for us is not to be compared with this life's sufferings. Beyond that is the wonderful news that we can have spiritual strength to endure trials when they strike our lives. Paul says that we do not face life's problems alone, but do so with the Holy Spirit through Christ in us. That's how Paul was able to remain assured in his terribly unsure years in prison. We should think of a spiritually joyful Paul in prison, not someone downcast and fearful.

Paul strides around in some small room in Rome, perhaps in the presence of or even chained to a Roman soldier. But Paul carefully dictates a profoundly positive letter to encourage the church (us). He writes hopefully of his future in spite of the obvious because he has seen Gods ultimate plan as it begins to unfold for you and me in the here and now! In Jesus, you have been chosen, handpicked for this purpose of being well able to live in His perfect will to the praise of His glory.

We became one with Jesus when we responded to the Word, the Gospel of our salvation. When we believed and received Jesus as our Lord and savior, we were marked in Him with the seal of Holy Spirit, who dwells within our heart. It is God's earnest guarantee to our inheritance in this life until the day when our total redemption is manifested to the praise of His glory and ultimate plan.

Chapter 11

Wisdom will guide!

~The greatest of all treasures await me,
and all I could ever hope to obtain
is mine if I only ask~

How much more successful can we become as willing partakers of God's plan for our life? Although there will those who content that learning how to succeed in life is wisdom. There are those who may disagree. Pleased in their present circumstance they believe their success is wisdom, but real wisdom comes from a spiritual existence. James 1:5 seems to confirm the importance of wisdom by saying "If any of you lacks wisdom, he should ask God, who gives generously to all without finding fault, and it will be given to him." James did not say, "If any of you lacks understanding" or "knowledge." He said, "Wisdom." This order is more then experimental, and following that order leads to wisdom releasing understanding. This, in turn, produces knowledge. Perhaps man should educate himself accordingly.

Thus, considered catching up with your spirit has been a matter of just asking for direction and guidance. Some things came to us out of necessity for life. Who wants to go around with their shoes untied or sit idly waiting on someone else to do it for you? When the availability of training has presented itself and is yours for the asking, the principle of catching up with your spirit is a necessity to build kingdom life skills. The wisdom of doing so has always been yours for the asking.

James 1:2 - 5 (KJV) *² My brethren, count it all joy when ye fall into divers temptations; ³ Knowing this, that the trying of your faith worketh patience. ⁴But let patience have her perfect work, that ye may be perfect and entire, wanting nothing. ⁵If any of you lack wisdom, let him ask of God, that giveth to all men liberally, and upbraideth not; and it shall be given him.*

Some find that it is much easier to declare or confer wisdom in or upon someone who looks or acts the part. It has not been limited to man or beast. There are no problems in existence for which God did not already create an answer. Paul was the solution to the problem, proving that

God can use anybody. David was the solution to the problem, and God used an outcast Joseph as the solution to the problem. When others turn their backs on our dreams, Jesus is the solution to the problem of your salvation, strength, and wisdom.

James wasn't the first to utter the phrase "wisdom." The Books of Job, Proverbs, Ecclesiastes, and Some of the Psalms are referred to as books of wisdom:

James 3:17 (KJV) *¹⁷But the wisdom that is from above is first pure, then peaceable, gentle, and easy to be entreated, full of mercy and good fruits, without partiality, and without hypocrisy.*

The word "wisdom" is not spoken of again until the angels sing it:

Revelation 5:12 (KJV) *¹²Saying with a loud voice, Worthy is the Lamb that was slain to receive power, and riches, and wisdom, and strength, and honour, and glory, and blessing.*

Wisdom is considered as one of the charismatic gifts. These gifts are so called because they are increasingly being manifested within the fellowship of believers around the world. They are sometimes called God's power tools, given to the body of Christ as valuable helps to accomplish works of ministry. Just as in the natural you wouldn't seek to operate power tools without training. *1 Corinthians 12:7 - 11 (KJV) [7]But the manifestation of the Spirit is given to every man to profit withal. [8]For to one is given by the Spirit the word of wisdom; to another the word of knowledge by the same Spirit; [9]To another faith by the same Spirit; to another the gifts of healing by the same Spirit; [10]To another the working of miracles; to another prophecy; to another discerning of spirits; to another divers kinds of tongues; to another the interpretation of tongues: [11]But all these worketh that one and the selfsame Spirit, dividing to every man severally as he will.* Wisdom is further listed the premier gift followed by, knowledge, faith, healing, miracles, prophecy, discerning of spirits, and tongues.

These gifts, when applied to our life, can be defined as **"A supernatural intervention of natural laws, bestowed by the Holy Spirit where His presence is invited and accommodated."** When you have Holy Spirit dwelling on the inside, wisdom can abide. Just ask for it.

The Anointing of Wisdom
Wisdom is not determined by your, age,
sex, or position.

ABIGAIL is a personal name meaning,
"my father rejoiced." She becomes the wife of
David after being the wife of Nabal, whose name
means foolish. The anointing of wisdom was
upon her, and she is praised for it because of her
husband's egotism in. 1 Samuel 25 David sent
out some men to Nabal, giving them authority
to use his name. Nabal is a large landowner and
a successful shepherd. He is holding a feast for
his sheep shearers while David is hiding from
Saul. David's request is simply for some food.
However, Nabal, in a drunken state, refuses the
request and insults David's ten messengers. In
anger, David decides to kill Nabal's entire household. Abigail anticipates David's reaction and
loads a convoy of donkeys with food to feed all
of David's men. As soon as she meets David, she
impressed him with her beauty, advice, humility,
and praise. *1 Samuel 25:32 - 33 (KJV) [32]And
David said to Abigail, Blessed be the LORD
God of Israel, which sent thee this day to meet
me: [33]And blessed be thy advice, and blessed be
thou, which hast kept me this day from coming to
shed blood, and from avenging myself with mine
own hand.* Abigail's wisdom saves a household.
There are still households where blessings have

been delayed. The head cannot act foolishly, unyielding, and believe everything will fall into place because the wife knows the King. He, too, has to establish a relationship with his unseen keeper.

Solomon indicated the need for wisdom when he said, "Wisdom is supreme; therefore get wisdom." *Proverbs 4:7 (KJV) ⁷Wisdom is the principal thing; therefore get wisdom: and with all thy getting get understanding.* Further, more, he said, "I, wisdom, dwell together with prudence; I possess knowledge and discretion." When God told Solomon, "Ask for whatever you want me to give you," Solomon answered, "Give me wisdom."

2 Chronicles 1:7 (KJV) ⁷In that night did God appear unto Solomon, and said unto him, Ask what I shall give thee. It seems that "wisdom" comes first, then understanding, and finally knowledge

Naomi the mother-in-law of Ruth spoke it to her daughter-in-law:

Ruth 3:3 - 4 (KJV) ³Wash thyself therefore, anoint thee, put thy raiment upon thee, and get thee down to the floor: but make not thyself known unto the man, until he shall have done eating and drinking. ⁴And it shall be, when he

lieth down, that thou shalt mark the place where he shall lie, and thou shalt go in, and uncover his feet, and lay thee down; and he will tell thee what thou shalt do. The Wisdom of the aged is much needed to be passed on to generations.

Esther used it wisely when she gained the king's favor:

Esther 5:1 - 8 (KJV) *[1]Now it came to pass on the third day, that Esther put on her royal apparel, and stood in the inner court of the king's house, over against the king's house: and the king sat upon his royal throne in the royal house, over against the gate of the house. [2]And it was so, when the king saw Esther the queen standing in the court, that she obtained favour in his sight: and the king held out to Esther the golden sceptre that was in his hand. So Esther drew near, and touched the top of the sceptre. [3]Then said the king unto her, What wilt thou, queen Esther? and what is thy request? it shall be even given thee to the half of the kingdom. [4]And Esther answered, If it seem good unto the king, let the king and Haman come this day unto the banquet that I have prepared for him.*

Job spoke of it as an excellent gift of God:

Job 28:12 (KJV) *[12]But where shall wisdom be found? and where is the place of understanding?*

Moses prayed for it:

Psalms 90:12 (KJV) *[12] So teach us to number our days, that we may apply our hearts unto wisdom.*

Joseph, Stephen, Daniel, and others were all of different ages, backgrounds and positions, but all were accounted for having wisdom

There is a difference between worldly intelligence and the anointing of wisdom. Presently, there is an ongoing conflict between the anointing of divine wisdom and understanding compared to the human or worldly view of wisdom and intelligence. Human wisdom tells us to get as much as we can, believe only what we can see, enjoy pleasure, and avoid pain.

God's wisdom tells us to give all we can, believe what we cannot see, enjoy service, and expect persecution.

Once the anointing of wisdom is upon you, the worldly pressures seek to overtake you. The apostle Paul was faced with a rather interesting dilemma:

First consider how he became an apostle *1 Corinthians 1:1 (KJV) [1]Paul, called to be an apostle of Jesus Christ through the will of God,* Secondly, He commended the church for having received spiritual riches, utterances, and knowledge, for it now has a testimony. *1 Corinthians 1:6 (KJV) [6]Even as the testimony of Christ was confirmed in you: Thirdly, He made plain that, let nothing divide you, because it is in the name of Christ that all are baptized*

With the church now growing and prospering, the only hindering factor to receiving wisdom is you. We find the apostle Paul in a church full of status seekers: Preachers, mothers, deacons, ushers, trustees, and life-long members.

Status seekers will never gain any recognition or status from the unbelieving world. The gospel, as Paul begins to explain, does not appeal to human pride; it cannot even co-exist with it. The gospel, however, as Paul informs the Corinthians and us, which suggest only one thing to do with pride-crucify it. Well, that sounds easy enough, but how do we put down what we have put up with all our lives? Simply put; use the anointing of wisdom

God lays out the solution and gives you the wisdom to make a choice, but self blocks us from using the anointing of wisdom received by means of the Spirit.

The tale of the man who thought he had achieved all God had for him but wanted more mirrors our own admission of having found our purpose.

Here lies his lesson.

This man longed to scale the top of the highest mountain in the world all because he assumed this would make him closer to the Lord. Therefore, he asked and prayed about this task and the means was made for his climb. After receiving little guidance, this man began his climb on a dreary morning. Slow and painstaking was his ascent, and finally upon reaching the top he began looking for God.

Unable to locate God, he became dejected because God neither spoke nor appeared, so he began his trip down. Halfway down the mountain, a storm came up, and his vision became blocked by the tempest like snowstorm. Suddenly, he felt he was lost, and fear set in.

The man slipped many times, but never lost his grip on the rope. Thinking the worst because he had lost his bearing, he began to pray to God for help.

The Lord heard and answered the man in a soft voice saying, "Let go of the rope!" The man, shocked at first, said, "Lord if I do I'll perish." Gods only reply was, "My Son, Let go of the

Rope!" However, he then began to depend on his own wisdom and the laws of physics.

The man began to cry and clung to the rope with all his might. The storm grew worst, and the night colder and darker. Before long, morning came, and during the night, the man died, frozen and still clinging to the rope.

As it would happen, a group of climbers happened along during their morning trip up the mountain and found the frozen man still holding to the rope. In amazement, one hiker asked why a man would die this way, holding on to a rope during a storm only three feet from the ground.

We are sometimes like the climber. When the wisdom of God comes to us, the obstacle of doubt and fear makes us afraid. When God says, "Let go, are you willing to let go? The anointing of wisdom can be yours, just ask for it! Self will keep you from knowing what God has for you.

Chapter 12

In the Course of

*~ Often taken for granted is the first
Steps of a child, but what is consummated in those
first few unsteady strives is the, Joy of success, the courage
to try and the willingness to move forward~*

It has been a foregone conclusion that some mindsets and attitudes have been altered, and some may seem impervious to these words of revelation. A renewed feeling will overtake you when you begin sharing these principles. There are those who will experience a Moses encounter in the pursuit of their spirit, but as you begin to lunge forward to the finish line "Your spirit" is re-energized. Break the tape and you see yourself standing before the promiser, much like Moses did unexpectedly: ***Exodus 3:2 - 5 (KJV)*** *²And the angel of the LORD appeared unto him in a flame of fire out of the midst of a bush: and he looked, and, behold, the bush burned with fire, and the* *bush was not consumed. ³And Moses said, I will now turn aside, and see this great sight, why the bush is not burnt. ⁴And when the LORD saw that he turned aside to see, God called unto him out of the midst of the bush, and said, Moses, Moses. And he said, Here am I. ⁵And he said, Draw not nigh hither: put off thy shoes from off thy feet, for the place whereon thou standest is holy ground.*

While standing on holy ground, there are those who must know and understand that holy ground will test your obedience. Be careful where you stand because while you're standing in the presence of the promiser, the promise will be spoken. For some, this may be their first spiritual connection. Those who had considered themselves once lost or confused are now called back into a relationship that was shaped years ago. It now becomes your redirection to finding your destiny. Out of the midst of your struggling, you may have yielded but did not forget the benefits of living wisely and according to God's word. Know that countless before you have undergone many of your same struggles, yet they made it.

Therefore, understand there are rules that govern your steps. In order to be successful in life, submit to them willingly. By your submission, your life will be lengthened by many years, and your prosperity will begin to overflow like a geyser in a desert land. Are you ready?

In this spiritual union to some or reconciliation for others, the finish line is where you now stand. In this spiritual place, a relationship was produced like any other relationship. It evolved from the courting process to the act of commitment and finally the consummation.

Much like Moses, you were born in a situation brought about by attempts to take your life. You drifted along, was found, and then lived according to worldly splendor. But God had better for you, and He began courting you.

The wonderful concept of courting involves committing an act or action that seeks to attract a person's attention. Things had to be done before you noticed. Remember the notes that were passed as children and asked the question, "Do you like me, yes or no? Check one." God also establishes the foundation of courting whereby trust and feelings are revealed, and the longing to be in that certain ones presence exists.

Moses, in his Egyptian surroundings, had never forgotten or may have never wished to forget, that he was a Hebrew." **You cannot change who you were born to be.** He resolved to make himself acquainted with the condition of his ancestry, and "went out among his brethren, and witnessed their burdens being many. During his excursion, what he saw was the cruel repression and bondage under which the people groaned.

God has a way of showing us where we really came from, and Moses had to understand like many of us that it had never been about him. His time had arrived for him to make a difference, and their cause was his vehicle of choosing. Moses may have thought that he could never make a difference in helping to break their yoke of bondage, but God had grabbed his attention. You cannot think about being selfish when God requires your moving because it is a decision where the choice is not yours. At first, you may choose not to do, but what happens to others in your family will eventually motivate you one way or another.

Moses made his choice accordingly. God was assuring that He would bless His promise for the welfare of his people. Moses, then left the palace of the king and took up his quarters, probably in his father's house, as one of the Hebrew people who had for forty years been suffering cruel wrongs at the hands of the Egyptians. He was no longer comfortable and could not remain undisturbed by the state of things around him. We notice the many signs of change and stand idle even if it's uncomfortable.

One day while among the people, Moses resentment showed against an Egyptian who was mistreating a Hebrew. He rashly lifted up his hand, slew the Egyptian, and hid his body in the sand. Many times, we remember things that we have done while upset, and we slay the memory of them thinking the secrets of our past stays hidden. How often have we said or heard, "What's done in the dark…"

The next day Moses found two Hebrews in an intense argument because of situational stress. He promptly found that his exploit of the previous day was no secret. His first reaction, like many, was to panic. "What if" attacked him as it does many when their past is questioned. Moses was concerned that his deed might reach the ears of Pharaoh. What really happens when the enemy hears your secrets? He thought Pharaoh would seek to slay him. Moved by fear, Moses fled from Egypt wandering and now wondering about his choice. But God was saying, "Do you love me? Check yes or no."

Moses found himself in the land of Midian, which means "strife." There have been situations of which we are certain that we were forced into action, where we have declared, **"This is it; I am not taking it anymore."** That is when the wonder of courting takes place. God uses these situations to guide us towards Him. **Ephesians 4:26 (KJV) says:** [26]*Be ye angry, and sin not: let not the sun go down upon your wrath:* Anger is the perfect tool of testing. We have been mad enough to strike, but we learn to forgive in spite of. We can avoid entering periods of darkness

(darkness being the territory of the enemy) and fleeing into the wilderness blindly.

God is waiting; He has resolved to make himself acquainted with our condition. What a test! God is courting us in order to form an alliance to engage in activities which lead to commitment. In the courting process, we communicate and there's enough contact with God, so He can commune with you. It is similar to absence from a special someone, and you still think about him or her. It means there's a commitment.

The commitment involves a charge or trust. The act of obligation or emotionally attachment, with such force it propels you into pursuit. When you have to go for it! Because there's an expected end. Moses goes into a stage of commitment; he finds himself in a situation where he again has to stand up for someone else. *Exodus 2:16-17* (**KJV**) *[16]Now the priest of Midian had seven daughters: and they came and drew water, and filled the troughs to water their father's flock. [17]And the shepherds came and drove them away: but Moses stood up and helped them, and watered their flock*. Moses has been taught that its not about him, because there are those in a condition trying to fight their way through a situation, and you can help. Are you committed? In pursuit, the reward of the promise often has unexpected results. Moses does not take a life, but marries Zipporah, one of the daughters. Unfamiliar to many is that from acts of kindness comes an emotional attachment that forms the union. After his commitment to change, he gains the trust of the family elder Jethro, the priest of Midian and is given responsibility. Moses then encounters God, and from this encounter, he finally understands the principal of taking his first steps.

Mose's life begins to line up with his destiny in these steps: **Exodus 3:1-5 (KJV)***[1]Now Moses kept the flock of Jethro his father in law, the priest of Midian: and he led the flock to the backside of the desert, and came to the mountain of God, even to Horeb. [2]And the angel of the LORD appeared unto him in a flame of fire out of the midst of a bush: and he looked, and, behold, the bush burned with fire, and the bush was not consumed. [3]And Moses said, I will now turn aside, and see this great sight, why the bush is not burnt. [4]And when the LORD saw that he turned aside to see, God called unto him out of the midst of the bush, and said, Moses, Moses. And he said, Here am I. [5]And he said, Draw not nigh hither: put off thy shoes from off thy feet, for the place whereon thou standest is holy ground.*

What about the path Moses chose and how does it compare to your transition to spiritual union? Moses, instead of following the normal route to the place of grazing, selects to travel through the back side of the desert. Understand that Moses learned many lessons while growing up in the house of Pharaoh and by position grew in favor in the sight of men, but also understand that when men see you mess up, they will not let you forget it.

Those who might have seen Moses (you) head off in another direction may have made comments about his past or whispered the gossip that they had heard. Moses may have countered ***Proverbs 2:20 (KJV)*** *[20]That thou mayest walk in the way of good men, and keep the paths of the righteous.*

Learn to walk in the ways of honorable men and women and select your role models wisely. Just because you see somebody do it one way doesn't make it right. If you ask, and they tell you how they did it and advise you this is what worked for them, you might need to make some adjustments. Then follow them and consider their counsel wise.

Moses was under a priest who trusted him with his flock. The Bible does not say, "and Jethro followed closely behind." *[1]Now Moses kept the flock of Jethro his father in law, the priest of Midian: and he led the flock to the backside of the desert,* Moses under ***Psalm 33:11 (KJV)*** *My Father's plans and purposes stand firm. They are settled in heaven for all eternity, I am confident that every one of His promises will be accomplished in my life.* Therefore, what people are saying contrary to the word of God cannot affect your destiny.

Moses was on course for his most valuable lesson, his Godly encounter. Two important things had occurred.

1. God is pleased when He finds us employed.

The second forty years of Mose's life were upon him. From birth he was raised in the palace and had others to care for him. Now at eighty (80), he had to work. Parents who receive us from birth change us, feed us, and teach us (that is your first forty). When you reach legal age, it's time for you to move on and gain employment for God and yourself. What happens is some think they can continue to live your first forty at home! **It is time to move on.**

Job 36:7-11 (KJV) the Lord's eyes never leave me. He keeps watch over all that I do and is my ever-present help to ensure my success. He corrects and disciplines me when I waiver and makes sure that I know what I have done wrong. He then sets me back on the path of His prosperity and sees to it that I spend my days in peace and contentment.

2. Being alone is a good friend to our communion with God.

"No one will get you out of trouble, but plenty will help you get in it."

2 Chronicles 33:12 (**KJV**) *¹²And when he was in affliction, he besought the LORD his God, and humbled himself greatly before the God of his fathers,* **When distressing days arrive, I remain humble before God and continually seek His favor.** Moses did two powerful things that drastically changed the course of his life when he saw the burning bush and heard God:

a. He entered into and followed God's personal call on his life.
b. He entered into a dynamic personal relationship with God the Father.

God is willing to show up in our lives, but what often gets in the way is that our own ability keeps us from turning aside. Look at these two things as the perfect 1-2 punch. Totally surrender your life to God the Father, ask Him to place you in His perfect will for your life, find out what your call and purpose is, and then do not be afraid to enter into a dynamic, powerful and personal relationship with God. If you are willing to do both of these things, I know God will take you into heights and destinations that are beyond what you could ever ask or think.

Psalms 119:27 (KJV) [27] *Make me to understand the way of thy precepts: so shall I talk of thy wondrous works.*

You are blessed with an intimate understanding of God's PRECEPTS. As you meditate on the word, then revelation knowledge is engrafted into your spirit.

PRECEPTS are principles, rules, or instructions that guide or stir your actions. Now, it serves as a warrant, a written mandate that is issued by legal authority.

Exodus 3:4-5 (KJV) *[4]And when the LORD saw that he turned aside to see, God called unto him out of the midst of the bush, and said, Moses, Moses. And he said, Here am I. [5]And he said, Draw not nigh hither: put off thy shoes from off thy feet, for the place whereon thou standest is holy ground.*

Moses was stirred to action not only by curiosity but also by a willingness to be obedient. Removing one's shoes has varying significance in Biblical history. One refers to those who refused to perform their duty in the case of taking their bother's wife in the case of his death: ***Deut 25:9***

(KJV) *⁹Then shall his brother's wife come unto him in the presence of the elders, and loose his shoe from off his foot, and spit in his face, and shall answer and say, So shall it be done unto that man that will not build up his brother's house.* Another involved redeeming your kinsman and staking new rights: ***Ruth 4:7 - 8 (KJV)*** *⁷Now this was the manner in former time in Israel concerning redeeming and concerning changing, for to confirm all things; a man plucked off his shoe, and gave it to his neighbor: and this was a testimony in Israel. ⁸Therefore the kinsman said unto Boaz, Buy it for thee. So he drew off his shoe.*

It is also used to represent a time of mourning: ***2 Sam 15:30 (KJV)*** *³⁰And David went up by the ascent of mount Olivet, and wept as he went up, and had his head covered, and he went barefoot: and all the people that was with him covered every man his head, and they went up, weeping as they went up.* Nevertheless, Moses was instructed to do so as a show of reverence.

Joshua did so when he was told: ***Josh 5:15 (KJV)*** *¹⁵And the captain of the LORD'S host said unto Joshua, Loose thy shoe from off thy foot; for the place whereon thou standest is holy.* We as children of promise have instructions that affect not only the elect: ***Psalms 33:8 (KJV)*** *⁸ Let all the earth fear the LORD: let all the inhabitants of the world stand in awe of him.*

The very entrance into the temple is mandated as we begin to worship and pay reverence: *Habakkuk 2:20 (KJV)* *²⁰But the LORD is in his holy temple: let all the earth keep silence before him.*

Once you begin to grow from these lessons, the Consummation comes. The completion of a union by means of close personal interaction is consummation. When you stand in reverence of God much as Moses did, your enemies are defeated.

Exodus 14:13 (KJV) *¹³And Moses said unto the people, Fear ye not, stand still, and see the salvation of the LORD, which he will show to you to day: for the Egyptians whom ye have seen to day, ye shall see them again no more for ever.*

God is with you, and the lonely nights are not as long as they once were. Tomorrow where you will stand a victory is promised

2 Chronicles 20:17 (KJV) *¹⁷Ye shall not need to fight in this battle: set yourselves, stand ye still, and see the salvation of the LORD with you, O Judah and Jerusalem: fear not, nor be dismayed; to morrow go out against them: for the LORD will be with you.*

Principalities are defeated and the once unreachable things are yours. Words spoken as, "Not at this time" or "We will get back to you," become. "We can help," and "you're approved."

Deut 7:24 (KJV) *²⁴And he shall deliver their kings into thine hand, and thou shalt destroy their name from under heaven: there shall no man be able to stand before thee, until thou have destroyed them.*

You stand in high places, and the hills are more inviting then intimidating.

Psalms 24:3 (KJV) *³ Who shall ascend into the hill of the LORD? or who shall stand in his holy place?*

It's written by God's hand and spoken by His word.

Isaiah 40:8 (KJV) *⁸The grass withereth, the flower fadeth: but the word of our God shall stand for ever.*

Although we all will not have the same kind of Moses story, many of us can definitely testify that all of our lives have been changed for the better and that our lives are exciting in God. God is no respecter of persons. Remember what happened to Moses once he surrendered his life over to God's call and then had enough courage and faith to enter into a very powerful relationship with God the Father. We see the miraculous occurring when the Lord calls your name to stand on Holy ground, victorious because of life lessons.

When you come to the place where you know you are supposed to be and you know the Lord has purposed to meet you there, be careful where you stand because it is Holy Ground, and your Spirit is caught.

The exposure to your **SPIRIT** empowers the perspective of human life when coupled with Holy Spirit, which is God's presence and power. It enables us to bear in the world and not dread but cause those to notice our presence.

Deuteronomy 2:25 (KJV) *²⁵This day will I begin to put the dread of thee and the fear of thee upon the nations that are under the whole heaven, who shall hear report of thee, and shall tremble, and be in anguish because of thee.*

One translation of Spirit is "wind," or "breathe." Jesus said that the Spirit is like the wind in that one cannot see it, but one can see its effects. This is true of both the Spirit of God and the spirit of a human being. United, they lead us into victorious living.

Conclusion

God is an unchangeable God. He has not altered the thing which has gone out of his mouth or called back one single consolatory sentence. Neither does He lack any power. It is God who made the heavens and the earth, who has spoken accordingly and made Spiritual apprehension, which had until now been an elusive charge for the Children of Promise. We have the comprehension of scriptures as:

Hebrews 12:23 (KJV) *²³To the general assembly and church of the firstborn, which are written in heaven, and to God the Judge of all, and to the spirits of just men made perfect,*

Zechariah 12:10 (KJV) *¹⁰And I will pour upon the house of David, and upon the inhabitants of Jerusalem, the spirit of grace and of supplications:*

When the will of God for all was established in the heavens, His word released to us healing in our time of affliction. When crisis approaches and chaos restricts us, our God, sends help. Our Spirit designates by divine nature as His eyes are always upon us. Through favor, and by heritage, we acquire delivery of the promise of God's word.

Deuteronomy 1:11 (KJV) *[11](The LORD God of your fathers make you a thousand times so many more as ye are, and bless you, as he hath promised you!)*

Abraham's blessing were the result of a promise. At the time of his receiving his precept he was not overflowing with the Holy Spirit. Yet he received the promise by showing himself faithful through his good works. Sometimes, you have to sow a little more than you're use to, or you have to pray for others that their Abram situations and circumstances will be changed to Abraham. Let the world know you live under the Promise, and when God says go, you go because it is your season. Whatever difficulties may be involved, God is rewarding the obedient and crowning the over-comer. In the keeping of them, there is great reward. God's promises ensure prosperity: **Psalms 19:11b:** *Then He shall reward every man according to his works*

The validity and reliability of God's word has assured us of success when we experience mis-understandings, difficult people, broken friend-ships, jealousy, and gossip. Do not allow these situations to become bars; you are of the promise. Break free and understand clearly. "You can declare," I will live, I am healed, I will prosper me and my whole house." Your spirit saw your hurts and pains, and you misunderstood as you were pulled towards victory and resisted. Now, with a new understanding, you have pursued it.

Scriptures support and strengthen our pursuit with words that sustain and provide exhortation. There are not only personalized to encourage those afflicted, but also designed to remind us that their affliction is noiseless and temporary when compared to the "far more exceeding and everlasting weight of glory."

We cannot be as the man promised an inheri-tance, placed in an invisible situation with the promise of a visible reward:

Word had come to a certain man that an inher-itance awaited him in a nearby kingdom. Eager to receive his promise, he arose early, mounted his donkey, and set off on his journey.

His only concern was making it to the kingdom where his inheritance was to be received. Not long into his journey, he encountered a young woman who was matted and bruised. As she stood before him, she told him of her mis-fortune and errors of her life. She explained how the many broken promises and abandoned dreams had shattered her Spirit. After years of following men who used her for their own pleasures, she was left hopeless. Her story brought tears to his eye, yet he offered no immediate help as his reply was, "I'm headed to the kingdom to receive my inheritance. Maybe if you're here when I return I can help you." Then he rode on. The road narrowed, twisted and turned. At points it was covered with biers and thorns, and yet he rode on.

A short time later, he came upon a man barely clothed and clearly broken in spirit. The man asked for a little water and food because all he had was lost through foolish living and plots to get rich. He heard the man say, "People said I'd end up like my father, worthless and good for nothing." The man heard this but, thinking only of his journey, offered no food or water, saying "I'm on my way to the kingdom to receive my inheritance. If you remain until I return, then I'll help." Again, he rode on.

Anticipating his inheritance, which lay ahead, was his only focus. He began to think of the many things his new fortune would bring. The sight of a man, a woman, and child traveling towards him halted his daydream. They looked exhausted as they walked slowly along the dusty path. The man once again halted his donkey. The *gentleman spoke of how they'd gone from town to town, wandering and seeking a better life. They suffered because people refused to forget their past and relayed stories of who they were and what they had been through. No matter where they settled, people would not accept them. This, many times over, troubled their Spirits. The man promised to help if he saw them once he received his inheritance and again rode off.*

*Finally, his journey was ending. The promise he sought lay just over a bridge. Onward he urged his donkey, but as they began to cross the bridge, it began to sink. So the man stopped and pondered his situation. The thought of his riches caused him to ignore the sign that read, "**Riders must get off before crossing.***

Once again, he inched the donkey forward, and again the bridge began to sink. Finally the man and his donkey both toppled over to their death.

Well, the man never got his inheritance, which is obvious, and if you noticed, he took the time to listen to people and their spiritual struggles but never helped. When he got to the bridge, all he had to do was walk over to the other side. Most of all, I like to make the most obvious point. You can get close to your inheritance, **but if you do not get off your donkey,** you will miss everything that is coming to you. Do not become the man in the story because your inheritance awaits you.

Your spirit has been enlightened with a flood of understanding, so you can now see and comprehend the hope of your calling. All things are placed under your feet, and every power and dominion must obey as you apply the power of attorney that Jesus has given you to use in his name. Jesus is to His promise found faithful even as God was to God's promises in sending this Child of Promise to the world.

About the Author

In *Catching up with your Spirit* International author, holistic counselor, and college educator Chris Avery express his passion for giving, sharing, and teaching. Because of his delight in disclosing the hidden truth and mysteries of the Word, he encourages others to do the same. His desire led to his motto, **"If the wisdom of the Word is not shared, then the knowledge is wasted, and the bridge of Hope is never crossed."** These words signify his desire to edify others through the revelations God allows him to inscribe.

Chris is the founder and Pastor of Revealing Grace Ministries Inc. He is also the principal host of a radio ministry airing in North Carolina. His Ministry reaches out globally while networking with others to serve many. He is a retired veteran who received high honors and ranking while serving the United States Army. Through the extent of his travel, whether in Europe or

Asia, he finds that truth and a need for hope, for humanity never changes. He is an alumnus of Central Texas College and Mount Olive College where he has earned degrees in human relations and counseling.

Loaded with wisdom and imperial declarations, *Catching up with Your Spirit* will prove to be of transitory value to its readers.

Breinigsville, PA USA
08 July 2010
241468BV00001B/14/P